Halting the Sexual Predators among Us

Halting the Sexual Predators among Us

Preventing Attack, Rape, and Lust Homicide

Duane L. Dobbert

Westport, Connecticut
London

Library of Congress Cataloging-in-Publication Data

Dobbert, Duane L.
    Halting the sexual predators among us : preventing attack, rape, and lust homicide /
Duane L. Dobbert.
        p.   cm.
    Includes bibliographical references and index.
    ISBN 0–275–97862–1 (alk. paper)
    1. Sex crimes—United States.   2. Sex crimes—United States—Prevention.   3. Sex
offenders—United States.   I. Title.
HV6592.D63   2004
364.4—dc22   2003056951

British Library Cataloguing in Publication Data is available.

Library of Congress Catalog Card Number: 2003056951
ISBN: 0–275–97862–1

First published in 2004

Praeger Publishers, 88 Post Road West, Westport, CT 06881
An imprint of Greenwood Publishing Group, Inc.
www.praeger.com

Printed in the United States of America

The paper used in this book complies with the
Permanent Paper Standard issued by the National
Information Standards Organization (Z39.48–1984).

10 9 8 7 6 5 4 3

Contents

Preface

Scenario #1

It had been a particularly long and cold winter, at least it seemed that way to John Doe. The gray sky seemed to have been there for months, and it felt like the Indian summer of last October was years removed. The lack of sunshine produced no natural endorphins. Only the videos kept John's urges at bay.

The ever-present urge was insistent. The need to touch and be loved was overwhelming. Alcohol, videos, and masturbation had kept the recurrent, intense arousal under control for the first few months, but the time had become too long. John could no longer wait. He could no longer be satisfied with just the thoughts of a youthful lover. The videos did not accurately portray his desired lover, and the visual stimuli were crude and often cruel and did not represent his love. It frustrated him that the children were of the wrong gender, race, and age. The sexual activity was commercial. It did not genuinely represent his love. The weather must change soon.

Waiting for the first day of spring, the warming temperature, and the annual advent of recess felt insurmountable, but John knew venturing early to the fence bordering the elementary schoolyard playground would be futile. No children would be at play.

It had also been a particularly long winter for fourth grade teacher Ms. Jones. The cold, snowy, and rainy weather had kept the children indoors for the past five months. Indian summer felt as if it had been years ago. Afternoons without outside recess had become unbearable. At a complete loss of further creativity, Ms. Jones awaited that first day of warm, dry weather with unbridled anticipation.

The nightly news predicted temperatures in the high 60s, perhaps the first sign of spring. Ms. Jones was delighted to hear the news of the warming weather and felt a sense of relief. The next day, the morning sun rose, fulfilling the forecaster's prediction, and the day began with excitement. Children debated with their mothers about wearing shorts instead of jeans, and Ms. Jones wore a spring dress. She greeted her students at the classroom door, excitedly announcing that the weather was to be sunny, bright, and warmer, and that lunch hour and afternoon recess would be held on the playground.

Meanwhile, John Doe took a shower.

Showering and shaving had been a once-a-week activity, only when John's predetermined weekend trip to the mall was at hand. He intentionally did not "clean up" before he ventured out to collect his unemployment check. John, fired from his job as a ticket taker at the local theater for making lewd comments to a young boy, had not worked since fall.

The elementary school was chaotic; children, teachers, aides, and even the principal could not wait for lunch and afternoon recess. John Doe could not wait either.

The location was predetermined. He had been there before, physically a few times, and mentally a thousand times. Arriving, he positioned himself against the playground fence with a perfect view of the soccer field. Only the fourth- and fifth-grade boys were allowed to play soccer.

The boys appeared from their classrooms; they pulled off their outer garments to reveal soccer uniforms. As strong, young, tender legs emerged, John Doe experienced the recurring, intense sexual arousal. Sustained through the long winter months by the videos, his flesh was now resurrected and the obsession rewarded with reality. Flesh that could be touched, fondled, tasted, and loved.

Ms. Jones, the aides, and the principal, elated that outside recess had arrived, contently watched the children at play, ignorant of outside observation. With their backs turned to the perimeter fence, they cheered as the soccer players madly dashed about the field, exuberant over the weather, ignoring the rules. John Doe, fingers intertwined in the chain-link fence, watched the scantily clothed players and selected his "dream lover." He initiated a plan to meet his lifelong fantasy lover.

In fulfillment of the predator's delusion, this young boy would love him unconditionally, forever.

Scenario #2

Friday finally arrived. Freshmen Megan and Heather had studied all week for finals, scheduled to begin on Monday. At nine in the evening, confident of their current level of preparedness, they decided to leave the university library and go to fraternity row where numerous prefinal parties were in full bloom. Concerned about the potential for sexual assault, they always traveled together at night. If circumstances found them alone on campus in the evening, they wisely requested a university escort.

With finals beginning on Monday, the pledges of one fraternity sponsored a keg party, and the chapter members were more than slightly intoxicated. The band arrived on time and all that was necessary was to await the arrival of the female students. Senior fraternity men Mike, Tom, and Joe spent the afternoon gearing up for the evening's adventure at the expense of the pledge class. Eager to become "actives," the pledge class had provided plenty of beer to the actives and "roofies" to a small but extremely influential group of seniors. These seniors were the guardians to active membership and expected special treatment. The pledge class decided on roofies, a date rape drug, as the special treatment.

Mike, Tom, and Joe, acknowledged senior actives, expected differential treatment. Fortified and uninhibited by an excessive amount of alcohol, they approached Megan and Heather, offering them cups of beer. Megan and Heather, excited over feeling ready for finals and their warm reception by the "big men on campus," accepted the cups laced with roofies. The desired amnesiac condition was produced. Armed with condoms, Mike, Tom, and Joe sexually assaulted Megan and Heather. Waking from the amnesiac and drunken stupor, Megan and Heather knew from the vaginal pain that they had been raped. However, without the condoms, the roofies, or witnesses, they could not identify their attackers.

These assaults were not only predictable, they were also preventable. These two scenarios are fictitious; however, assaults of this nature occur in every community in the United States.

Yet, we wait.

We wait until the sexual assault occurs. We fail to recognize the existence of precursor behaviors. The behaviors demonstrate sexual disorders that precipitate the final assault. Perhaps it is not a failure to recognize, but rather a form of denial. If our heads are conveniently submerged in the sand, we can display our outrage rather than confess our ignorance and naiveté, or acknowledge the relationship between the precursors and the assault. Our fear of the liberal defenders of individual rights thereby allows sexual predators to commit heinous crimes against the innocent. Apathy is the real culprit here. Society takes the attitude that if the precursor behavior is not being committed in our neighborhood, it only exists elsewhere or simply does not exist at all.

However, sexual assault can exist in any neighborhood in America. It is ignored in the affluent communities, depicted by the media as a lower socioeconomic phenomenon. Yet it is alive and flourishing in the best of the communities, acknowledged only when the assault becomes a forcible rape, child abduction, or homicide.

Since the late 1970s, the Behavioral Sciences Unit of the Federal Bureau of Investigation has been collecting data on serious violent crime. The Violent Criminal Apprehension Program (VICAP) solicited collaboration with state, county, and local law enforcement agencies in the collection of data on such crimes. As the data bank grew, a statistically significant fact emerged. In excess of 90 percent of the serial murders were lust homicides. Lust homicides are those committed by persons who, while committing the homicide, demonstrate behavior indicative of a sexual assault. The homicide was secondary to the sexual assault, or it was directly attributable to the motive, which was sexual in orientation and demonstration.

It is logical to assume that sexually disordered persons committed the crimes. Further, it is significant to indicate that lust homicide is not the first manifestation of the individual's sexual disorder. The recurrent, intense sexual arousal was present much earlier than the assault. The recurrent sexual arousal was not dormant, but rather was demonstrated in less obvious and less heinous behaviors. The characteristics of the assault were also apparent in previous behaviors demonstrated by the sexually disordered person, but due to ignorance, reluctance, and fear, society neither identified nor acknowledged these behaviors.

This book explicitly demonstrates that the sexual assaults society chooses to recognize and acknowledge are only the most serious behavioral manifestations of sexually disordered persons. These persons have acted upon their disorders previously, in less offensive and allegedly lawful fashions. This book is a wake-up call to potential victims, parents of potential victims, and professionals who are mandated with the responsibility of protecting potential victims and apprehending perpetrators.

This book is intended for multiple audiences—for lay readers and academics. Consequently, it uses clinical terminology but does not assume prior expert knowledge. It carefully defines and describes mental health, personality, and sexual disorders. The classifications are those that appear in the *Diagnostic and Statistical Manual of Mental Disorders, Fourth Edition, Text Revision* (DSM-IV-TR) (2000), published by the American Psychiatric Association. This book will utilize these medically established and legally recognized classifications and their respective diagnostic criteria, but it will take them a step further by offering "lay" definitions and descriptions.

One of the values in offering the established classifications, descriptions, and diagnostic criteria as well as lay versions is that nonclinical people can become familiar with the correct terminology. It is common for nonclinical people—including legal, law enforcement, education, and other human services personnel, as well as the media—to use terms that are inaccurate. Even the most educated individuals refer to someone as "crazy" when the person has not been diagnosed with any form of mental illness. Understanding the correct terminology with the addition of lay definitions and descriptions assists us in clearly communicating with one other.

This book specifically discusses sexual paraphilias, sexual disorders, stalking patterns, sexual assaults, and lust homicides. More importantly, it examines the relationships of the disorders to the illicit conduct. While the latter may be more remote, the prior behaviors commonly coexist, and progress from paraphilias through sexual assaults.

The material contained in this book is a compilation of this author's experiences during thirty-plus years as a criminal justice clinician, educator, consultant, and forensic examiner. It is based on the research of hundreds of clinicians, researchers, and criminal justice practitioners. It has been tested in the field with law enforcement and in the academy and university classroom.

It is the author's hope that this book finds its way on to the desks of professionals in many disciplines, university professors, and students, as well as the nightstands of parents. The motivation to write this book grew out of the appalling number of sexual assaults and abducted children, the vast proliferation of pornography that influences illicit behaviors, and the lack of knowledge regarding the relationships between prior behavior and sexual assault. The intent is to enlighten potential victims, parents of potential victims, and the professional community assigned the responsibility of preventing the occurrence of sexual assault.

Acknowledgments

This book would not have been possible without the great personal sacrifice, uplifting support, and gentle prodding of my dearest companion and friend, my wife Joyce Elaine Dobbert. She was a constant inspiration through this process and she believes in the importance of this book as passionately as I do.

To Carole Greene, thank you for your support. You were an instant friend and your outstanding editorial expertise was extremely important to this book.

To Suzanne Young and Nicole Fizer, thank you for your assistance in preparing the manuscript.

The author also wishes to acknowledge the work of the staff and the volunteers of the National Center for Missing and Exploited Children. Their dedication has increased the recovery rate of missing children from 60 percent in the 1980s to 91 percent in 2001. A percentage of the author's profits from this book has been pledged to this valuable organization.

Parts of this manuscript have been reprinted with permission from the *Diagnostic and Statistical Manual of Mental Disorders, Fourth Edition, Text Revision.* Copyright 2000 American Psychiatric Association.

Part I

SEXUAL PARAPHILIAS

Chapter 1

Introduction

The National Center for the Victims of Crime (NCVC) (2001) reported that in 1998, 103,845 children, or about 1.49 children per 1,000, were sexually abused. The NCVC also reported that in 1999, the overall crime rate dropped; however, there was a 20 percent increase in rape and a 33.3 percent increase in sexual assaults. Thirty percent of the victims did not know the attacker.

Further statistics compiled and reported by NCVC (2001) indicate that in the kidnapping of children 17 years or younger, 27 percent involved nonfamily acquaintances and 24 percent involved strangers. The National Women's Study (1992), conducted by the National Center for the Victims of Crime, reported that 683,000 forcible rapes occur each year, which equals 56,916 per month, or 1.3 per minute (http://www.ncvc.org).

This reporting of sexual assault, rape, and lust homicide could continue ad nauseam to no further purpose. The reality of sexual assault, rape, and lust homicide has been recognized and documented for decades. These data are reported here to urge the reader to understand that the problem is not fantasy, nor is it minor. It is a social problem of immense proportion, and society has been unsuccessful in decreasing its frequency and deterring the conduct. Although incarceration rates increase, the rate of offense is unaffected.

Obviously the solution to the problem has escaped us. Therapeutic interventions, incarceration, involuntary mental health commitments, and chemical castration have not made a dent in the incidence of sexual assault, rape, and lust homicide. Resolution of this heinous problem lies in a fresh examination and response.

The etiology of sexual assault is controversial. Clinical, law enforcement, and judicial practitioners disagree as to the etiology and, consequently, the social response. Mental health practitioners identify clinical disorders as the etiology of the conduct, while criminal justice practitioners suggest the etiology is found in control and violence. They do, however, agree on the same point: No current interventions successfully decrease the incidence of assault or deter persons from performing the behavior.

This book suggests that the motivation for sexual assault, rape, and lust homicide is unique to the attacker; the motivations are as authentic as the attackers. Some persons assault, rape, and commit lust homicide for control and domination. Others engage in the same behaviors based on motivation that is inherent to sexual disorders. These disorders are referred to as *paraphilias*.

More importantly, in most episodes of sexual assault, rape, and lust homicide, the motivation for the attack is demonstrated in the manner in which the attack was performed. This assumption stems from the theory that all behavior is motivated by stimuli that is internal and external to the attacker and the victim. In simpler words, the attack happens for a reason; there is purpose and intent. If there were no purpose for the behavior, then the behavior probably would not happen. Therefore, it is critical to ascertain and examine the motivation that precipitated the attack.

The final premise of this book that supports this fresh look at sexual assault is that in the majority of all incidents, precursor behaviors existed that may have predicted the assault. It has been repeatedly established, empirically, that prior behavior is the best predictor of future behavior. In retrospect, one can identify precursor behaviors that were predictive of the more serious behavior. A punch that is thrown in a domestic violence dispute is preceded by threats of harm and demonstrations of violence against inanimate objects. Throwing an ashtray through a window during an intense argument is a behavior that has purpose. The motivation to throw the ashtray is to demonstrate anger and the threat of harm: "It is an ashtray now, but it could be you next. I am capable of hurting you." The behavior intends to threaten and stop the intense argument.

Unless a person has an immediate and unexpected psychotic break, all behavior can be predicted by his or her previous behaviors. A rational, mentally healthy person performs behavior because the behavior meets his or her needs. If there were no purpose for the behavior, it would not be performed. The American Psychiatric Association in the *Diagnostic and Statistical Manual of Mental Disorders, Fourth Edition, Text Revision* (DSM-IV-TR) (2000) identifies purposeless and disorganized behavior as a primary diagnostic criterion of Schizophrenia (p. 300). Consequently, purposeful behavior is expected of persons not afflicted with Schizophrenia and related forms of mental illness.

Behavior has purpose. It is motivated by stimuli. Anger and aggression can serve as the motivators in a domestic violence dispute; the attacker selects a behavior to vent his or her anger and aggression. It is rare when no indications of this potential behavior were evident from previous encounters. Therefore, the behavior may be predicted, and if it can be predicted, it can be prevented.

This same set of premises can be applied to sexual assault, rape, and lust homicide. These activities or behaviors are precipitated by motivation. If the motivation can be ascertained, the future behavior can be predicted. A person who commits rape has performed inappropriate sexual conduct in less serious behaviors before the rape. His precursor behaviors may have included forced petting with a victim and peeking into the windows of people's residences in hopes of finding them undressing, bathing, or engaged in sexual activity. He may have followed an attractive woman as she goes about her daily business. He may have called her telephone and left no message just to hear her voice or voice message. The attacker's precursor behavior meets his needs; he will continue this behavior as long as his needs exist.

Many of the behaviors discussed in the previous paragraph are identified as sexual paraphilias in the DSM-IV-TR. If the individual experiences "recurrent, intense sexually arousing fantasies" (p. 566) regarding these behaviors, he is demonstrating the diagnostic criteria of a paraphilia. These behaviors are directly precipitated by the specific paraphilia and can produce "interpersonal distress and interpersonal difficulty" (p. 566). This distress and interpersonal difficulty may be shown in behavior that is illicit criminal activity. These behaviors may also be predictive of future behavior and/or a progressive pattern leading to serious criminal offenses.

It is extremely important to note that not all persons who are diagnosed with a sexual paraphilia will commit criminal behavior. Many seek therapeutic intervention to resolve their interpersonal distress and interpersonal difficulty. Others choose to find consensual partners with whom to engage in their sexual paraphilia. However, when an individual acts on a sexual paraphilia in a way that violates the criminal code, it must be acknowledged and dealt with accordingly.

This book will thoroughly examine the criteria of sexual paraphilias that may be linked to sexual assault, rape, and lust homicide, and it will explicitly describe their potential behavioral manifestation.

Chapter 2

General Characteristics

Webster's Unabridged Dictionary (2001) defines sexual as "1.) of, pertaining to, or for sex; 2.) occurring between or involving the sexes" (p. 1755), and it defines paraphilia as "a type of mental disorder characterized by a preference for or obsession with unusual sexual practices" (p. 1409).

In comparison, the American Psychiatric Association in the current DSM-IV-TR (2000) defines paraphilias as "recurrent, intense sexually arousing fantasies, sexual urges, or behaviors generally involving 1) non-human objects, 2) the suffering or humiliation of oneself or one's partner, or 3) children or other nonconsenting persons that occur over a period of at least six months" (p. 566).

As a collaborative definition, *sexual paraphilia* may be considered an abnormal or irregular sexual activity that includes recurrent, intense, sexually arousing fantasies, sexual urges, or behaviors that involve nonhuman objects, suffering of oneself or partner, or children or nonconsenting adults. We may consider a person afflicted with a sexual paraphilia one who experiences intense, sexual arousal based on fantasies or behavior associated with inanimate objects, children or nonconsenting adults, and/or actions of masochism or sadism (involving inflicting pain on oneself or others). The most critical aspect of the aggregate definitions is the recurring, intense, sexually arousing response to the desired stimuli. The stimuli may be inanimate, youthful, or nonconsenting, or emotions, like shame, that are directed inwardly or outwardly. The thought or the presence of the stimulus produces intense, sexually arousing responses. The sexual arousal produces other behaviors.

The intensity of the stimulus and the satisfaction level of the response to the stimulus determine the comfort level of the disordered person. If the stimulus is high and the response is insufficient, the arousal continues, and the disordered person experiences frustration and increasing anxiety. If the response to the stimulus satisfies the individual's fantasy or desire, the urge subsides. If you recall from the preface of this book, our John Doe's anxiety escalated until his fantasy was played out.

While all individuals experience sexual fantasies and may engage in self-stimulation to reduce the sexual desire, individuals diagnosed with sexual paraphilias experience intense desires and fantasies recurrently. After masturbation or sexual activity with a consenting adult, nondisordered persons return to a level of comfort. The fantasies become dormant for a varying amount of time, depending on the individual and the availability of consensual sexual activity. Individuals who engage in frequent sexual activity experience sexual urges more often than individuals who engage in sexual activity less frequently.

Human development psychologists indicate that sexual activity peaks at different ages by gender. It is also generally accepted that after these peaks of sexual activity, libido decreases with age. "With advancing age comes a reduction in the production of sperm and seminal fluid, in the number of orgasmic contractions, and in the force of the ejaculation" (VanderZanden, 1997, p. 462). Some adults over 50 succumb to the social belief that they are too old to have sexual desires, and if aging males are not stimulated over long periods of time, their responsiveness may be permanently lost (Masters & Johnson, 1966).

The fantasies and desires of persons diagnosed with paraphilias occur much more frequently and intensely than those of the nondisordered person. "Many individuals report that the fantasies are always present" (DSM-IV-TR, p. 568). Masturbation does not return the individual to a calmer state, free of the fantasy desire. "Sexual paraphilias tend to be chronic and lifelong" (p. 568). Gratification is achieved through orgasm, but is short lived, as the fantasy desire returns quickly. The more chronic the paraphilia, the more frequent the need to act upon the fantasy or desire, and the more rapidly the urge recurs.

The American Psychiatric Association is quick to indicate that these intense, recurring sexual fantasies, desires, and urges are only to be considered paraphiliac "when they lead to clinically significant distress or impairment" (p. 568). Individuals who cannot continue mainstream social activity without experiencing the intense sexual arousal are experiencing distress and impairment. Individuals are impaired when these periods of arousal cause them to change their daily activities. Individuals are impaired if they engage in illegal behavior because of the influence of these fantasies. Individuals are impaired when their life activity is consumed with behaviors due to the intense sexual arousal.

The frequency of the intense, recurring sexual arousal is also influenced by stress. Psychosocial stressors influence everyone in different ways. Individuals experience physiological, emotional, intellectual, and sexual reactions to stress-producing situations and anxiety-producing thoughts. Physiological responses include shallow and rapid breathing, increase in body temperature, increase in blood pressure, and increased secretion of digestive fluids. These physiological responses to stress are temporary in cases of acute stress and the body quickly returns to a calmer, less agitated state. Exposure to chronic stress may precipitate long-term physical implications such as illness, disease, and anatomical dysfunction.

Emotional responses to anxiety may be short lived in cases of acute stress. In contrast, chronic stress may produce long-term serious emotional impairment, including Posttraumatic Stress Disorder, with recurring symptoms that affect daily functioning. Cognitive responses to psychosocial stressors may include forgetfulness, indecisiveness, and an inability to rationally process information.

Psychosocial stressors also influence feelings of sexuality and intimacy. Individuals who experience chronic stress tend to lose their desire for intimacy. Individuals are most apt to encourage and enjoy intimacy when they are comfortable with themselves and their environment. A stress-free environment is conducive to feelings of intimacy. Conversely, feelings of intimacy are uncommon when an individual is faced with anxiety-producing situations.

Individuals diagnosed with sexual paraphilias, in contrast to nondisordered individuals, are more apt to experience increases in the recurrent, intense, sexually arousing fantasies, urges, and desires as psychosocial stressors increase. In nondisordered persons, the desire for intimacy is inversely related to psychosocial stressors. As psychosocial stressors increase, the desire for intimacy decreases, and vise versa.

Persons diagnosed with sexual paraphilias are the exact opposite. A direct relationship exists between the level of psychosocial stressors and the recurrent, intense sexual arousal. As psychosocial stressors increase, the recurrent, intense sexual arousal increases, and vice versa.

This characteristic of sexual paraphilias is significant to our examination of the relationships of the disorders and the behaviors associated with sexual assaults. This chapter will next look at other characteristics of all the paraphilias and their relationship to assault behavior.

It is important to stress that some behaviors, fantasies, and objects associated with paraphilias do not always indicate a diagnosis of sexual paraphilia. Some of these behaviors, fantasies, and objects are not pathological, but are utilized as a stimulus for sexual excitement. Pornography that features bondage does not dictate a sexual paraphilia if it is used by two consenting adults for sexual stimulation and if it does not produce clinically significant distress or impairment. Consensual adults who view a pornographic film or video of sexual bondage as a means to become sexually stimulated, and who subsequently simulate the bondage in the video, are not necessarily demonstrating the criteria for a diagnosis of a sexual paraphilia. However, if one of the partners obsessively utilizes the bondage or the viewing of the bondage in order to achieve sexual stimulation, then a diagnosis of sexual sadism may be appropriate. It is critical to understand that a fantasy, behavior, or object standing alone does not dictate a diagnosis of sexual paraphilia. Clinically significant distress, impairment in social relationships, behavior forced upon a nonconsenting adult or child, or legal complications are necessary to document the diagnosis.

Increases in the intensity of the level of stimulation may not be a symptom or characteristic common to all the paraphilias; however, it is a significant issue for forensic examiners. Not all individuals diagnosed with a sexual paraphilia will require an increasing level of stimulation, but persons whose sexual behaviors compel them to act beyond the parameters of law frequently have the common characteristic of requiring higher and higher levels of stimulation. This characteristic is significant in the determination of recidivism of the behavior. Research has repeatedly demonstrated that—and I will say it again for emphasis—prior behavior is the best predictor of future behavior, and this guides forensic examiners in the prediction of recidivism and required levels of stimulation.

Case studies of serial killers who commit lust homicides demonstrate that the time between homicides decreases and/or the requisite level of stimulation demonstrated in the homicides increases. Kenneth Bianci, the infamous "Hillside Strangler," committed numerous lust homicides in Los Angeles, California, and King County, Washington. Studying the chronological sequence of the known murders, it becomes apparent that there were few common characteristics of the victims. Unlike Ted Bundy, who, with the exception of the Chi Omega Sorority murders and the 13-year-old victim in Florida, stalked and murdered young women who looked remarkably similar, Bianci murdered women and girls of different ages, races, and appearance. His victims superficially appeared to be random. Closer analysis demonstrates that Bianci's recurrent, intense sexual urges required his increasing the intensity and the different types of stimulation. Shortly after his spree of killings began, he was no longer satisfied with sexual assault and murder, and he began to experiment with varying forms of torture of his victims. Bianci also experimented with women of different races, young girls, and then, eventually, with multiple victims at the same time. Bianci's trail of lust homicides ended in his conviction in King County, Washington, for the murder of two women, who, after being raped, were tortured and then murdered by hanging in a staircase. Other lust serial killers have demonstrated a similar pattern of behavior requiring heightened levels of stimulation.

Jeffrey Dahmer, following his arrest and conviction, stated that he was looking for the most beautiful young men, regardless of their age or race. Dahmer searched for his perfect fantasy lover, one who was beautiful and would remain with him forever. With his increasing desire to find the perfect lover, he experimented with alcohol, drugs, and exotic forms of sex. On at least one occasion, Dahmer attempted to conduct a partial lobotomy on one of his drugged victims by drilling a hole in his head and pouring acid into the hole. His attempts at creating sexual slaves or zombies failed. His dismembering of the bodies and preserving the genitals and heads of his lovers demonstrated his increasing need for heightened stimulation. His experimentation with cannibalism was a behavioral manifestation of his escalating need to have his lovers always be a part of him.

The examination of victimology, lapses of time between assaults, and increasing levels of heightened stimulation, as indicated in sadism and torture, is critically important in the prediction of future paraphiliac behavior and victims.

As was previously indicated, sexual paraphilias commonly exist in a co-morbid state. An individual may exhibit the symptoms of more than one paraphilia. These co-existing or "comorbid" paraphilias may be progressive and demonstrate a logical increase in stimulation. The individual may no longer become sexually aroused by the pornographic video of a sexually sadistic act, and may require increased stimulation to attain the same level of satisfaction. The need for increased stimulation may require deeper levels of degradation or torture in a video format, or may precipitate a personal encounter. The simulation of sadism may be insufficient and the individual may take his needs beyond the confines of his living room and television. He may search for a prostitute or masochistic partner. This heightened need for sufficient stimulation and gratification is critical to the prediction of sexual assault.

The following is a significant criterion utilized by forensic examiners. The American Psychiatric Association in the DSM-IV-TR indicates, "except for Sexual Masochism, where the sex ratio is estimated to be 20 males for each female, the other Paraphilias are almost never diagnosed in females, although some cases have been reported" (p. 568). Some women are diagnosed with sexual paraphilia, *however, compared to the number of men diagnosed, there is really no statistical significance. Therefore, probabilities dictate that males are more apt to possess sexual paraphilias than females.* This statistic delineates the unknown suspect group of a sexual assault to a suspect group of males.

The most significant general characteristic to forensic examiners and criminal investigators is that "*the individual paraphilias can be distinguished based on differences in the characteristic paraphiliac focus*" (emphasis added) (DSM-IV-TR, p. 569). Later chapters in this book will discuss individual paraphilias and their unique characteristics, but it is this single, general characteristic—common to all paraphilias—that sheds critical light on the investigative process. Individual paraphilias are distinct from one another, and the behavioral acts that stem from them are unique. Consequently, an individual diagnosed with Pedophilia will exhibit behavioral manifestations that are unique to Pedophilia. A pedophile will purchase pornographic material that is characteristic of his paraphiliac focus—naked children, rather than naked adult women or men, engaged in sexual activity. He will stalk his fantasy object in groups where they congregate—elementary playgrounds, not college women's soccer games.

The recurrent, intense sexual arousal is particular to the paraphiliac focus, and not to all paraphilias. This characteristic is the most critical element in the identification of sexual predators and the prevention of sexual assault.

The following chapters will discuss the sexual paraphilias as identified by the American Psychiatric Association. To reiterate, many paraphilias exist together and often reflect a progression from less to more intense behavioral manifestations.

Chapter 3

Exhibitionism, Fetishism, Frotteurism, Voyeurism

EXHIBITIONISM

Scenario

The high school cheerleaders emerge from the gymnasium giddy with excitement over the pending rivalry on the football field. The sun has set and the playing field 200 yards ahead of them is ablaze with lights. The atmosphere is electrified by the presence of fans on both sides of the field.

They approach the field from around the varsity baseball dugout. Two of the girls straggle behind the group and are surprised by the presence of a man standing in the shadows of the dugout. He calls out to them to ask directions to the ticket booth and as they turn to answer him, he opens his trench coat and exhibits his erection. The girls scream and run to the field and he stealthily mingles with hundreds of fans. The brief encounter is sexually fulfilling to this man who is afflicted with the disorder of *Exhibitionism.*

Exhibitionism Defined

"The paraphiliac focus of Exhibitionism involves the exposure of one's genitals to a stranger" (DSM-IV-TR, p. 569). Various aspects of the behavior of exposing one's genitals must be taken into consideration of a diagnosis of Exhibitionism. It is critical that in Exhibitionism, as in all the other sexual paraphilias, the generic qualifiers be acknowledged:

1. Recurrent, intense sexual arousal
2. Clinically significant distress or impairment in social, occupational, or other important areas of functioning
3. Violations of law, in some cases
4. Specific requirements for erotic arousal

Going in alphabetical order, Exhibitionism is the first of the paraphilias, and it demonstrates adherence to the generic diagnostic criteria for all sexual paraphilia.

Actually displaying one's genitals does not automatically mean Exhibitionism. If ever the fantasy of exhibiting one's genitals is intensely sexually arousing, then a diagnosis of Exhibitionism may be appropriate. However, other displays of one's genitals do not qualify for a diagnosis of Exhibitionism. It is critical that the DSM-IV-TR criteria be acknowledged when evaluating instances of individuals' displaying their genitals. For example, it is doubtful that exotic dancers experience intense sexual arousal while exposing themselves to their customers; it is reasonable to assume that these dancers experience little or no sexual arousal, and are performing their acts because it's a lucrative, tax-free career. Similarly, the fraternity member who "moons" the freshman dormitory is not exhibiting his genitals because he feels intense sexual arousal from the activity, but rather because of his sophomoric mentality. It is critical to consider the motivation of an individual's exposure.

If an individual exposes his genitals to an unsuspecting stranger while masturbating, a diagnosis is obviously appropriate. If the exposure is intended to attract a stranger into an intimate relationship, then a clinical diagnosis may be appropriate. If the conduct occurs repeatedly, then a diagnosis is appropriate. The DSM-IV-TR also suggests that the act of exposing is not what is sexually arousing to the individual. The fantasy—that the viewing of his genitals will sexually arouse the observer and an intimate relationship may develop—is what sexually arouses this person. Thus, the act of exposing one's genitals is moved by different motivations, and the motivation for the behavior is significant.

Commonly referred to as "flashers" are those individuals who, under the cloak of a long raincoat, are naked and expose themselves in crowds. If the stranger's victims are relatively random and are not characteristically similar, with the exception of gender, the exposing behavior may be for shock value, alcohol-induced, or perhaps a symptom of another disorder.

For example, one of the common characteristics of Schizophrenia is grossly disorganized behavior. This symptom may show itself in a variety of behaviors. "The person may appear markedly disheveled, may dress in an unusual manner (e.g., wearing multiple overcoats, scarves, and gloves on a hot day), or may display clearly inappropriate sexual behavior (e.g., public masturbation)" (DSM-IV-TR, p. 300). Generally, schizophrenics are harmless to others, but their behavior and appearance make them seem otherwise. The bus station and subway dwellers frighten us, and we avoid them. When a disturbed individual exposes himself and masturbates in public, we scream "pervert" and think "sexual predator." Usually they are not. They are just disturbed, but this is a lesson that only a minuscule percent of the population will ever learn.

As will be discussed in further chapters, the behavior of exposing one's genitals to a stranger may not be the paraphilia Exhibitionism, but rather part of the behavior pattern of a more severe sexual paraphilia. It may also be an early behavioral manifestation of a different sexual paraphilia, with the individual progressing through steps toward the ultimate fantasy objective. In this case, the act of exposing one's genitals is not the recurrent, intense, sexually arousing fantasy, but rather one behavior in a set showing a different paraphilia.

FETISHISM

Scenario

The middle-aged man finds himself sitting directly across from the display window of the Victoria's Secret store and longs to touch the lacy, silk panties of the women in the posters. He cannot find the courage to enter the store and touch the lingerie because some well-meaning sales clerk will accost him with inquiries like, "Can I help you find something in particular, Sir?"

The adjacent JC Penney department store is crowded with customers and the sales clerks are too busy to ask him if they can help. Husbands are standing about, bored and embarrassed, while their wives pick through the sale lingerie. His presence is not as obvious as it would be in the Victoria's Secret store. He quickly locates silk panties and then walks across the aisle, picks up a man's shirt, and gets in line to check out.

He takes his treasures home and experiences a growing erection as he pulls the panties from the shopping bag. He examines the silky material, smells it, and masturbates with the panties caressing his penis. He might ask his sex partner to wear the panties in tonight's encounter. He is obsessively infatuated and sexually stimulated by this inanimate piece of clothing. This man is afflicted with the paraphilia of *Fetishism*.

Fetishism Defined

The diagnostic criteria for Fetishism are the same as those for Exhibitionism. Similar to the discussion of Exhibitionism, it is also critical that the specific behavior associated with Fetishism be carefully analyzed. Fetishism can exist as a singular sexual paraphilia, as comorbid with another sexual paraphilia, or as one of a set of behaviors requisite to another sexual paraphilia.

> The paraphiliac focus in Fetishism involves the use of nonliving objects (the "fetish"). Among the more common fetish objects are women's underpants, bras, stockings, shoes, boots, or other wearing apparel. The person with Fetishism frequently masturbates while holding, rubbing, or smelling the fetish object or may ask the sexual partner to wear the object during their sexual encounter. Usually the fetish is required or strongly preferred for sexual excitement, and in its absence, there may be erectile dysfunction. (DSM-IV-TR, p. 569)

One must evaluate additional considerations before a diagnosis of Fetishism can be determined. The onset of Fetishism is usually during adolescence, when adolescent males are also simultaneously undergoing puberty. They are preoccupied with their own sexual anatomy and inquisitive regarding the female anatomy. Preadolescent males explore the new sensations stirring in their groin. They self-stimulate by lying on the floor and grinding their genitals into the carpet while watching television, and they secretly watch their mother or sisters for an opportunity to view the female genitalia.

It is not a sexual anomaly for an adolescent male to secretly play with his mother's or sister's undergarments. In fact, it is common and expected behavior of an adolescent male's pubescent exploration. They search through the laundry for worn female undergarments, fondling the silky texture and smelling the fabric for the "scent of a woman." These behaviors are neither perverse nor indicators of future sexual predators. Masturbation that involves the mother's or sister's garments and viewing pictures of naked women is normal and expected.

An uninformed parent will not recognize the natural inquisitiveness of the pubescent male. Victorian attitudes about sexuality and masturbation convey to the "offending" adolescent that his fantasies and behaviors are abnormal, evil, and perverted. As the behavior continues, the adolescents' guilt grows. A healthier parental response is to educate the youth regarding the nature of sexuality and the privacy of the practice. While the secretive behavior of masturbating with a fetish object should be discouraged, punishment for the behavior should be carefully considered. If the youth steals the fetish item, then punishment for the theft may be considered appropriate. Horror stories of parental responses to fetishes abound. Serial killer John Wayne Gacy was found wearing his mother's undergarments, and as punishment, his father made him wear girl's clothing to school. Henry Lee Lucas, who has admitted to more than 200 serial lust homicides, was also forced to wear girl's clothing to school. This is not to suggest that being forced to wear girl's clothing in public precipitated the development of their serial behavior, but merely to demonstrate parental overreaction to fears of Fetishism behavior.

Further, it is necessary to determine if the sexual arousal merely pertains to the inanimate object, or if there is a corresponding relationship with the anatomy associated to the article of clothing. In the previous chapter, the concept of the general characteristics of sexual paraphilias was discussed. The DSM-IV-TR (p. 569) informs us that the paraphilias can be distinguished from each other based on the focus of the paraphilia. Individuals with sexual paraphilia collect items that are directly distinguishable to the paraphilia.

An excellent example of this differentiation is the inanimate object—a woman's shoe. On the surface, it seems obvious that an individual who collects women's shoes and admits to masturbating in them is thought to have the Fetishism paraphilia. However, other aspects of the behavior might indicate a different paraphilia. If all of the shoes are boy's shoes with sizes common to 6- to 8-year-old boys, the collection of these shoes might be a requisite and precursory behavior of the sexual paraphilia Pedophilia. A pedophiliac commonly collects objects of clothing that are relevant to the age and gender of his preferred fantasy lover. These shoes may have been stolen from little boys of the victim group.

An alternate explanation is that the shoes belong to a particular person with whom the collector is obsessive. Before her marriage to Donald Trump, Marla Maples' apartment was illegally entered and the burglar stole only her shoes. When the thief was later apprehended, it became obvious that this individual did not have a shoe fetish, but rather a delusional, obsessive compulsion for Marla Maples. The obvious inquiry was "Why shoes and not more intimate articles of clothing?" It is probable that Ms. Maples washed her undergarments but not her shoes, and her scent was more detectable in her shoes. The individual probably stole shoes that helped him fantasize about a sexual encounter with Ms. Maples. I suspect that the shoes were stiletto heels rather than running or tennis shoes; the heels fulfilled his image of Ms. Maples, as depicted in the media, as a beautiful, seductive woman.

Continuing with the shoe as a potential fetish object, another alternative can be considered. As we proceed to understand all the sexual paraphilias, it will become increasingly evident that individuals position themselves closely to the focus of their paraphilia. Consequently, one could conclude that shoe sales clerks may have a fetish for shoes. On the other hand, the individual may have the sexual paraphilia Partialism, which is a less common paraphilia of "exclusive focus on part of the body" (DSM-IV-TR, p. 576). The individual may experience recurrent, intense sexual arousal with the feet of people. The shoe is not the sexually arousing stimuli, but rather people's feet are.

Because women's clothing is a common inanimate object of Fetishism, the subject of cross-dressing must be considered. "This Paraphilia is not diagnosed when the fetishes are limited to articles of female clothing used in cross-dressing, as in Transvestic Fetishism" (p. 570), which will be discussed later. A man who dresses in women's clothing for purposes of transvestic activities experiences recurrent, intense sexual arousal not from the inanimate clothing object, but from the motivations associated with transvestism. The individual diagnosed with Fetishism has recurrent, intense sexual arousal from a particular piece or type of clothing. This person incorporates this fetish in his sexual encounters as well as for self-stimulation. He may choose to wear the garment or require his partner to wear it during sexual activity. The fetish may be requisite to sexual arousal and failure to use it may result in penile dysfunction.

In summary, it must be recognized that a diagnosis of Fetishism is more complex than merely a determination that an individual is collecting inanimate objects that provide him with sexual stimulation. The behavior may be indicative of a much more serious paraphilia and comorbid with a personality disorder.

FROTTEURISM

Scenario

The business day has ended and thousands of commuters scramble to the subway, anxious to get home. The subway platform is crowded to the point of being dangerous to stand too close to the edge. Too short to see over the heads of the tall men, a middle-aged woman is trapped in the crowd. Like a cork bobbing in the surf, the woman is pushed and pulled by the movement of the sea of people. She uses both arms to hold her purse tightly to her chest, knowing that this is the perfect opportunity for a would-be purse snatcher.

Suddenly she feels two hands groping her buttocks and thighs. Unable to turn around and swat the probing hands, she cries out, but her cries are muffled by the approaching train. The swelling mob pushes her along into the train. When she turns around there are dozens of men in close proximity, none of them looking directly at her. She does not know the identity of the person who assaulted her.

Standing on the platform, the guilty man awaits the next rushing group of commuters. He will play out the same act numerous times before the rush hour is over. This is the lifestyle of the man afflicted with *Frotteurism*.

Frotteurism Defined

"The paraphiliac focus of Frotteurism involves touching and rubbing against a non-consenting person" (DSM-IV-TR, p. 570). Similar to the other sexual paraphilias that have been discussed, the definition of Frotteurism must meet the five general criteria outlined in the definition of Exhibitionism.

The DSM-IV-TR discusses behavior that is typical for a consideration of Frotteurism. Individuals diagnosed with this paraphilia have the recurring habit of rubbing their genitals against an unknowing and nonconsenting person in crowded locations such as subways, buses, and crowded streets. Some may use their hands to fondle the breasts, buttocks, and genitals of nonconsenting persons. While performing the behavior, they fantasize that the victim is consensual and enjoying the caress. This behavior intensifies their sexual arousal.

Again, it is important to consider the circumstances surrounding the behavior. The DSM-IV-TR suggests that the onset of Fotteurism occurs in adolescence and that the majority of the individuals afflicted with it are between the ages of 15 and 25 years (p. 570). It is further suggested that the behaviors associated with it decline with age.

It is not surprising that the behaviors would appear during puberty, as young men fantasize of sexual encounters and masturbate. The ultimate fantasy of young men as they proceed through puberty is to explore the female anatomy with their hands or to stimulate their own genitals by rubbing against the thigh or buttocks of a nonconsenting woman. If acted upon, this behavior generally results in a negative sanction, and as the woman screams, the woman or bystanders may assault the young man in return. Young men apprehended for this behavior are commonly referred to a juvenile court for sexual misconduct. The act in itself is brazen and requires significant courage for an adolescent to commit.

Adolescents are more apt to commit the behavior as a dare from other adolescents or with a date. Adolescent females often demonstrate their interest in intimacy as they, too, explore their sexuality through things like the self-examination of growing breasts and genitals. They fantasize about sports and music "heroes" and stimulate themselves to experience the new pleasure. Their budding sexuality also includes competition with other adolescent females, and unfortunately, many adolescent females judge themselves according to their popularity with boys, particularly boys who are older than they are. They want to wear make-up and dress like the model, actor, and singer divas whom the boys are drooling over.

The combined effect is obvious. A young man cannot wait to fondle a girl's breasts and genitals. A young girl cannot wait to demonstrate her superiority over peers because an older boy has asked her out to a school event or the theater. While the young man's goals are nearly universal, the young girl is interested in experiencing her first kiss but not petting. Their goals are different. When the young man fondles his nonconsenting date, the response from the young girl may take any of several forms. She might merely rebuke his advance or she might cry out in fear. She might retaliate by assaulting the boy or she might even tell her parents that the boy sexually assaulted her.

For many years every young man and young woman has similar experiences repeatedly through the dating process. Thus the inquiry: Is the recurrent, intense sexual arousal of petting indicative of Frotteurism? Of course not; however, many young men have ended up with a serious criminal record as a sex offender for this behavior, and many young women have ended up with tainted reputations because they do not rebuke the advances but instead encourage the intimacy.

One may seriously question the validity of the incidence and prevalence suggested in the DSM-IV-TR. The paraphilia does exist independently or comorbid with other paraphilias, or it may be a precursor of more serious paraphilias. The difficulty in consideration of this paraphilia lies in the potential for more serious sexual assault as part of a more severe sexual paraphilia. The behavior can be excused as just "boys being boys." On the other hand, failure to recognize the behavior as a recurrent, patterned behavior can result in recidivist sexual assault.

The prevalence and typical age group as suggested in the DSM-IV-TR may also be challenged in relationship to reporting. Young men who fondle or rub their genitals on nonconsenting persons will be reported as perpetrators of sexual assault. Men in their senior years who do the same thing are rebuked but then excused as "dirty old men." They are not reported to law enforcement agencies as perpetrators of a sexual assault. However, failure to attach a consequence to the behavior results in the reinforcement of that behavior.

The reward for fondling is extremely positive to the person who is doing the touching. He now has a tactile memory to associate with his fantasy, and he will revisit the experience as he masturbates. A fantasy of the victim's enjoying the intimacy is also present in the mind of the disordered person. When the behavior is not reported and virtually excused, the victims also set themselves up for further potential encounters with the same offender. The offender has found his fantasy lover; it is no longer necessary to find someone else. If the assault takes place on a bus or a subway, the offender will return the next day, at exactly the same time, to find his fantasy lover. If the victim is assaulted while commuting at a regularly scheduled time and mode of transportation, she will become a victim of the same man's stalking behavior. Even if the individual does not attempt to fondle her again, his fantasy is still reinforced: "She came back. She loves me too."

Recurrent Frotteurism activity with different victims may indicate that paraphilia or it may occur in direct correlation with a more severe paraphilia. If the recurrent behavior is with young boys or girls, it may also be indicative of Pedophilia.

Frotteurism must be viewed as a sexual assault, regardless of whether it appears to be the misdirected act of an exploring adolescent or a senior citizen. It is, in fact, a sexual contact with a nonconsenting person. It is not merely watching the intended victim; it is a hands-on assault. It is a considerably more brazen act than observing or purchasing pornography. It is an assault, and in the absence of a negative sanction, the behavior will be repeated. Further, if the individual finds the pleasure of the act more compelling than the negative consequence for the behavior, the behavior will continue. If the sexual predator who fondles the nonconsenting person is apprehended and receives a sanction that is insufficient in deterring him from further acts, he will learn a lesson: how to modify his approach and methodology to reduce the possibility of detection and apprehension. He will become better at his trade. His modus operandi will mature as he narrowly escapes apprehension.

The recurrent, intense sexual arousal associated with the rubbing or touching is ever present in Frotteurism. The person's fantasy requires increasing levels of stimulation and the act that previously produced stimulation may no longer feel satisfying. His drive becomes more demanding and the hunger to find the consensual lover pervades his being. His assaults become more brazen, his acts more intrusive—and it is the actions that distinguish the focus of the specific paraphilia. If his victims appear to be random, and no victim pattern emerges, then the diagnosis of Frotteurism is probably accurate. If he searches for victims with specific age and gender characteristics, then the Frotteurism behavior is probably a symptom of a more serious paraphilia.

VOYEURISM

Scenario

The sun set hours ago, the late news is over, and the apartment lights are shutting off one by one. The evening is hot and muggy and most of the apartment dwellers, college students and young working couples, have left their windows and drapes open in hopes of finding a cool breeze amid the summer humidity. Air conditioning is a luxury that exceeds their budgets.

Dressed in black jeans, a dark long-sleeve sweatshirt, and a black cotton watch cap, a man moves silently at the back of the buildings, sneaking from shadow to shadow. He has darkened his face with army-surplus camouflage paint. He has been to this complex during daylight hours and has determined which are bedroom windows and which are bathroom windows. He approaches an apartment where the light has just been turned out. He cautiously peers inside the bedroom window, hoping to find a couple engaged in sex or someone in a stage of undress.

Moving from apartment to apartment, he is finally rewarded with the view of a young woman sleeping naked above the bed covers. He removes his penis from his pants and masturbates as she sleeps unaware of his presence. He will return tomorrow night, as he has adjusted his work schedule so that he can be available to venture out every night. This man is a voyeur, more commonly known as a "Peeping Tom."

Voyeurism Defined

According to the DSM-IV-TR:

The paraphiliac focus of Voyeurism involves the act of observing unsuspecting individuals, usually strangers, who are naked, in the process of disrobing, or engaging in sexual activity. The act of looking ("peeping") is for the purpose of achieving sexual excitement, and generally, no sexual activity with the observed person is sought. Orgasm, usually produced by masturbation, may occur during the voyeuristic activity or later in response to the memory of what the person has witnessed. Often these individuals have the fantasy of having a sexual experience with the observed person, but in reality, this rarely occurs. (p. 575)

Similar to the other paraphilias, a diagnosis of Voyeurism requires the presence of the generic qualifiers. A person is considered afflicted with this paraphilia if he has recurrent, intense sexual arousal from observing strangers naked, disrobing, or engaging in sexual activity. In analyzing Voyeurism, it is necessary to evaluate it as an independent sexual paraphilia, as comorbid with other paraphilias, and as a requisite behavior of a more serious sexual paraphilia.

While Voyeurism is often diagnosed as an independent paraphilia, very often a Voyeuristic behavior is a symptom of a more serious paraphilia. Voyeurs are individuals who actively engage in peeping in the windows of others in hopes of finding the victims naked, disrobing, or engaged in sexual activity. If this activity is recurrent and intensely sexually arousing, and the individual has fantasies about a sexual relationship with the victim, then a diagnosis of Voyeurism is warranted, particularly if the victims appear to be random.

Many individuals who reside in high-rise apartments purchase telescopes to look into the windows of other apartments. Under the guise of stargazing, these individuals turn out the lights in their apartment and search the adjacent buildings for a view into others' apartments.

While this behavior certainly can be considered intrusive, offensive, and perverted, it is not usually considered Voyeurism. The clinical definition of Voyeurism requires the intense sexual arousal, fantasy, and social impairment. If an individual is preoccupied with the activity, modifies his social and occupational life in order to engage in peeping, is intensely aroused in anticipation of a find, and then masturbates while watching, the diagnosis is probably valid. Individuals who change their work and social habits to be home at the correct time for viewing are probably voyeurs.

In contrast, individuals often engage in this same high-rise-apartment activity as a social event. Cocktail party hosts who leave their telescopes in open display next to their living room windows are encouraging their guests to join in and experiment with this voyeuristic activity. Some couples may utilize these viewing events as stimulation for their own sexual engagement. It is similar to watching pornographic videos, except that the persons being viewed are in the flesh and are unaware of the observers. The Hollywood production *Sliver* portrays the use of a telescope during a cocktail party as a social event, as well as the voyeuristic behavior of Sharon Stone's character.

A voyeur without access to a telescope or a high-rise apartment resorts to sneaking from house to house or around the exterior of apartment complexes searching for windows with open curtains. These individuals may dress in dark colors and camouflage their face in order to get close to the building without detection. Under the cover of darkness, they may even carry small collapsible ladders to access bathroom windows that are commonly constructed above normal ground-level observation. The clandestine nature of this activity is also sexually arousing to the voyeur. If the act of watching nonconsenting persons naked, disrobing, or engaged in sexual activity was in itself sexually stimulating, the individual would simply watch pornographic movies while masturbating. It is the intrusiveness and stealth that enhance the intensity of the sexual arousal. Civilian access to night-vision glasses has increased the boldness of existing voyeurs, and has probably precipitated an increase in the number of individuals involved in voyeuristic activities.

The definition of Voyeurism can be extended beyond the DSM-IV-TR criteria to include a variety of other activities. If the act of watching others naked, disrobing, or engaged in sexual activity is sexually arousing, then one must consider reading pornographic material and watching pornographic videos, exotic dancers, and "live sex" shows as forms of Voyeurism. The only difference is that these activities are often legal and not intrusive. The logical questions are: Do intrusive, illegal, voyeuristic behaviors progressively develop from legal, less intrusive behaviors? Or does the individual just wake up one morning and decide that tonight he is going to peep in the windows of unsuspecting victims? Logic dictates that the precursor behaviors did exist.

Some individuals who do not have consensual sexual partners use pornography for sexual satisfaction. The market for legal pornographic material is enormous and the volume of illegal pornographic material cannot be estimated. Voyeuristic individuals begin by purchasing legal forms of pornography and, as they hide behind drawn curtains, watch these videos and masturbate. The enormity of the market alone suggests that the individuals purchasing pornographic materials are buying them in quantity, and that they desire variety. Interviews with known sex offenders have demonstrated that these individuals require ever-increasing, heightened levels of stimulation to produce the desired intense sexual arousal. Just as an addict requires higher and more frequent doses of heroin to support his habit, the sexual paraphiliac requires higher levels of perversion to stimulate his sexual arousal. When legal forms of pornography no longer produce the desired effect, the paraphiliac's obsession forces him to cross the line from legal to illegal, and the deviance is now criminal. But what does the budding voyeur do when the illegal print and video pornography no longer produce the desired result? The voyeur must view flesh "live" and not on the television.

The first, most logical, and legal method of viewing naked and disrobing women or men is to patronize bars and clubs featuring exotic dancers. Bars and clubs are available for all sexual preferences, and they provide their patrons a sense of anonymity. The voyeur is very satisfied to sit quietly in the dark corners of the bar drawing no attention to himself. Other patrons arrive in groups and demonstrate sufficient boisterous, drunken behavior to ensure his anonymity. He is able to stay for hours, after having met the requisite cover charge, to watch naked men or women and sustain his intense sexual arousal. If the corner is dark enough and if he is undisturbed by the half-naked servers, he might attempt to masturbate through his clothing. Or he might sneak off to the privacy of a stall in the men's bathroom.

Interestingly, the raucous nature and atmosphere of the bar can also drive the voyeur away. The male or female dancers who ply their trade for tips are completely aware that they are being observed and exploit the customer's observation to increase their tips. The dancers tease and taunt the customers, allowing them to slip currency into their G-strings. The dancers make their greatest revenue by lap dancing. The customer pays a large fee for the exclusive right to have a dancer gyrate her body, as naked as legally allowed, on the customer's lap. The dancers dance on stage and on laps without discrimination; money alone buys the performance. As a voyeur observes, he fantasizes that the observed party is his lover, but all fantasies of a monogamous lover disappear in an exotic bar or club. The true voyeur steps outside of the legal environment and into the illegal one in search of the "forbidden view" and monogamous fantasy love.

Commonly socially inept, the sexually disturbed voyeur finds it difficult to establish a sexual relationship with a consenting adult. The voyeuristic behavior eliminates social awkwardness and the darkness of night reduces the potential of being detected. The only inherent danger is that in order to observe, he must approach residences where the lights are on because the residents are awake, and consequently, alert.

Civilian access to night-vision glasses has eliminated the dangerous aspect of voyeuristic activity. Now under the cover of total darkness, the voyeur can approach a residence that is dark without having any light with him. This becomes even more valuable for the voyeur because particularly in warm climates, people open their curtains or shades after they have turned off the lights. Voyeurs also know that couples tend to engage in sexual activity in the dark. Night-vision goggles have enhanced the activity of voyeurs and decreased the privacy and safety of the public.

Night-vision glasses or goggles normally appear in catalogues for outdoorsmen and militia. Their recent appearance in catalogues selling pornographic paraphernalia demonstrates that voyeurism has become high tech. Before the availability of night-vision glasses, voyeurs had to begin their foraging during the hours when most adults are still awake. At such times community members are out taking their dogs for late evening walks, dogs are still in yards before being brought in for the night, and people are coming and going from late night activities. Success in peeping was contingent not only on stealth, but also on careful planning.

Some neighborhoods are more approachable than others, and even more so on certain days of the week. Determining this requires premeditated reconnaissance during the daylight hours. Voyeurs actually stalk a neighborhood during the daylight hours, identifying the best locations, directions of approach, channels of escape, and houses with the highest potential for success. The secretive nature of the reconnaissance is as exciting as it is frustrating. In order to reduce detection, neighborhoods needed to be evaluated. The advent of night-vision glasses has eliminated some of that necessity. Daylight reconnaissance is done only to identify locations where suitable victims reside and to ascertain the likely presence of a dog. A barking, or worse, a biting dog, is the voyeur's first enemy.

The voyeur selects a few houses that he believes are relatively secure from dogs and weapons. Signs on the front and back doors that say "This house is protected by Smith and Wesson" are a definite deterrent to would-be voyeurs. However, such a sign often functions as a welcome mat for burglars who are looking for residences to break and enter in the absence of the owner. This assures them of the availability of weapons to fence.

The modern voyeur dons his night-vision glasses and begins his journey during the hours when everyone is in for the night. He approaches the first residence—chosen as his prime location—and ascertains if the shades or curtains are open or closed. The bedrooms in homes are generally identifiable from the outside and are often at the back of the house. The voyeur approaches with stealth and peers into the window of the dark room, hoping to find someone naked, disrobing, or engaging in sexual activity.

If the voyeur finds a residence where his intrusive peeping is successful, he will then masturbate. After the "show" is completed, the voyeur—armed with a vivid memory—returns to his home to recall, fantasize, and masturbate again. Similar to the heroin addict, the voyeur will return the next night for his "fix." The voyeur will continue to use this particular house unless he is detected, finds the curtains drawn, or becomes bored with this particular victim. However, every successful peep at the same house and the same victim reinforces his fantasy that this person is in love with him. The voyeur delusionally believes that the observed person actually knows she is being observed, consents to his observation, and awaits further contact.

If a voyeur becomes fixated on a particular victim, he will eventually require a higher level of stimulation for his sexual arousal. The delusional belief strengthens his resolve and begins to reduce his inhibitions regarding social contact. The voyeur will make plans to meet his fantasy lover. He will discontinue his foraging of neighborhoods and will begin to concentrate exclusively on his "lover." The plan requires further reconnaissance.

While there are numerous mechanisms to find out a particular resident's identity, the intrusive nature of reading her mail accomplishes two purposes: It identifies her and provides other intimate information about her. The stalk has begun. The voyeur has progressed from voyeuristic behaviors to obsessive-compulsive behaviors. He has become a serious sexual predator.

He will begin daylight visitation to ascertain his victim's schedule. When does she leave for work, what is her mode of transportation and when does she return? To acquire this information, he merely strolls through the neighborhood. He may wear generic work clothes or obtain a uniform from a local utility company. The busy neighbors pay little or no attention to the alleged utility company employee as he strolls down the street. After carefully watching for indications of detection, he removes her mail from her mailbox, slips it inside his shirt, and continues his stroll.

Returning to his home, he uses these new items of intimacy to produce intense sexual arousal. He masturbates over the mere thought of them. He reads her name, studies the contents of her mail, and learns personal information about his "lover." Her phone bill provides him with her phone number as well as phone numbers of people she has called long distance. Catalogues and magazines provide additional insight into the woman's interests. If the catalogue is addressed to her personally and not to "patron" or "resident," the voyeur presumes she has requested it and that it says something about her lifestyle. Cooking, gardening, outdoor sports, and other categories of catalogues expand his fantasy horizon. Catalogues for exotic island vacation packages and Victoria's Secret intimate garments overwhelm him, and the sexual arousal becomes extreme. He envisions them together at a resort hotel, her dressed in a Victoria's Secret intimate outfit. His arousal levels climbs, his masturbation occurs more frequently, and his need to contact her becomes a compulsion.

Despite his compulsion and the intense sexual arousal, the voyeur knows that if he strolls the neighborhood and steals her mail every day, he will be detected. He also wants contact to be on his terms, to be assured that she is not frightened by his intrusive behavior. He will continue his night-vision visits to her house to look for an item of her clothing. An unlocked side door to the garage or an unlocked screened patio is the opportunity he desires. Clothing missing from the clothesline is obvious and will result in investigative inquiry. However, a forgotten T-shirt or dirty shorts from gardening left in the garage are less apt to be missed. Trash cans often contain junked personal items as well as discarded mail. Trash cans also contain intimate items, such as soiled menstrual pads, the ultimate treasure.

Subsequent progression will include following her as she departs for work. Where does she work, what does she do, whom does she talk to? The "stalk" has intensified. As disgusting and perverse as this scenario may seem, it describes the world of the voyeur and the sexual predator.

The definition of Voyeurism must be expanded to include all nonconsenting observation. A voyeur is not just a person who lurks around in the dark peeping into people's windows hoping to find someone naked, disrobing, or engaged in sexual activity. It is a person *visually* stalking others.

Webster's Unabridged Dictionary (2001) defines voyeurism as "the practice of obtaining sexual gratification by looking at sexual objects or acts, esp. secretively" (p. 2133). The elderly man who sits in Central Park and watches couples lying on blankets kissing is a voyeur. If it were not pleasurable, he would not watch it. The young man who intently watches little league soccer players take off their warm-up suits is a voyeur. He is deriving great pleasure from this activity. Men who stroll the beaches looking for young women wearing thong bikinis are voyeurs.

As long as society continues to define Voyeurism only by the criteria established by the American Psychiatric Association, sexual predators will progress to more severe sexual paraphilias. Even if Voyeurism is an independent paraphilia, it will become comorbid with other paraphilias unless it is detected and stopped. It will increase in intensity and the paraphiliac behavior will increase in severity.

It is unreasonable to think that we can write statutes and subsequently enforce laws prohibiting the act of observing people who have not consented to their being observed. However, it is reasonable for members of society to individually inquire, Why is that man watching those children take off their soccer warm-up suits? Why is that older man sitting in his beat-up, old pickup truck watching those children leave the elementary school and get on the bus? Does he have any legitimate reason to be parked and watching these children? If he is not waiting to pick up a child and take her or him home, why is he parked there? Many older men do take their children and grandchildren home from school, however, many men observe children because it is pleasurable to do so, and this behavior can be construed as Voyeurism.

In the fall of 2000, a 6-year-old girl was abducted at the site of a little league soccer match. The sidelines were full of enthusiastic little league parents and grandparents cheering on the players. One grandfather was videotaping the game and the police secured the tape from him to see if he had inadvertently taped the abduction. Unfortunately, the abduction was not on the video; however, the law enforcement agents were able to identify five known, registered sex offenders standing on the sidelines, watching the match. None of the five offenders had children or acquaintance with children playing in the match. They were there watching the match because it was pleasurable to do so. These men were utilizing voyeuristic activity as part of their more serious paraphilia.

It is reasonable for a police officer to stop and talk to a man sitting in his car watching children play or exit school. It is not only reasonable, it should also be a general order that suspicious persons found near schools, parks, playgrounds, and malls be stopped for inquiry as to their identification and reason for being in that particular location. Recording of the incident, the person's identity, and his automobile license number is a reasonable expectation for law enforcement.

Likewise, it is a reasonable expectation that teachers and principals call 911 to report suspicious persons watching children play at recess, at soccer matches, and at swim team practices. Bus drivers should be expected to write down the license plate numbers of suspicious vehicles and turn them in to the principal, who in turn should report these to local law enforcement. The simple questions of "Who are you?" and "What are you doing here?" will go a long way to deter sexual predators and establish a record of their inappropriate presence.

Every state in the union has passed a mandatory registration and reporting law similar to Megan's Law. The effectiveness of these laws in deterring sexual predators from recidivist behavior is contingent upon society's reporting the suspicious presence of persons. The number of law enforcement and corrections personnel in the United States is inadequate to provide surveillance of sexual offenders. Society, too, must assume the reporting function.

Telephone Scatologia, Necrophilia, Partialism, Zoophilia, Coprophilia, Urophilia, Klismaphilia

Chapter 2 discussed the general characteristics common to all sexual paraphilias and Chapter 3 was devoted to sexual paraphilias that have a greater incidence and, when independent of other paraphilias, are less serious. The final discussion in Chapter 3 implies that these paraphilias become more serious if they exist comorbid or progress to more serious and severe paraphilias. Chapter 4 will discuss sexual paraphilias that are rare in comparison to the ones previously discussed, and that are commonly associated with other diagnoses. These paraphilias have strange and perverse characteristics.

As in the criteria of all of the paraphilias, the same set of characteristics is requisite to a valid diagnosis of the paraphilias discussed in this chapter.

The following paraphilias are identified in Section 302.9, "Paraphilia Not Otherwise Specified," in the DSM-IV-TR (p. 576). This is far from an exhaustive list and *any* focus that precipitates recurrent, intense sexual arousal that meets the criteria listed previously for sexual paraphilia would be considered as such. While the following may appear strange and aberrant to the reader, these paraphilias are not fictitious. They are clinically recognized sexual disorders. The annals of abnormal psychology and law enforcement document the existence of these paraphilias. They are frequently referred to as *exotic*, meaning "strikingly unusual or strange" (*Webster's Unabridged Dictionary*, 2001, p. 679). However, fascinating and interesting should not be construed as alluring but rather, disturbing. Persons who perform some of these paraphilias are seriously and clinically disturbed.

TELEPHONE SCATOLOGIA

Scenario

He adjusts the pillows on the bed, turns the sensual music to the perfect volume, and carefully positions his drink, the telephone, and the photograph of the beautiful naked woman. Everything must be exactly right before he places the call. He dials the 900 number and anxiously awaits the voice answering the phone. The anticipation is sexually stimulating.

Finally, he hears the seductive "Hello, darling. How can I help you this evening?" His rehearsed, sexy-sounding greeting is disrupted by his sexual arousal and his voice squeaks in a pubescent tone. She masterfully describes how she is dressed and how she has been awaiting his call. She encourages him to take off his clothing as she takes off hers, piece by piece, ever heightening his state of arousal. She describes the fondling of her breasts and vagina and tells him that she feels like it is his hands, not hers. She describes her approaching orgasm and tells him to hold on longer. She asks him to imagine her lips caressing his penis. The longer she can keep him on the phone without orgasm, the more money is added to the credit card account he has given her. Finally, he ejaculates. In a final gesture of affection, she asks him to call back tomorrow.

This man is afflicted with *Telephone Scatologia* and will continue to call back until the credit card is cancelled for failure to pay.

Telephone Scatologia Explained

The focus of this paraphilia is obscene phone calls. Initially, it was a diagnosis reserved for individuals who make obscene phone calls to strangers. These individuals experience intense sexual arousal by making a phone call to a stranger and using obscene language during the very brief conversation. The response of the victim intensifies the sexual arousal and the caller masturbates as he recalls the victim's response. If the victim of the call does not hang up and continues to listen or responds with her own diatribe of obscenity, the caller's behavior is reinforced because he believes he has found a lover. Recognizing the nature of this reinforcement, the best defense against a person who is making obscene calls is to interrupt them and ask them to call back at a designated time later in the day so that they can talk privately. The caller has two possible responses: agree to call back at the designated time or quickly hang up because he knows that if he calls back his call will be traced. The intensity of his sexual arousal and his experience as a caller will dictate his reaction. Regardless of the caller's reaction, the victim must immediately report the call to the phone company, which will immediately prepare for the return call. Making an obscene phone call is a federal offense and the phone companies have a blanket authorization to record and trace such a call. Within a few seconds of the next call, the company will have sufficient evidence for the request of an arrest warrant. This technology has significantly reduced the number of obscene calls to stranger victims. However, other technology has increased the practice of Telephone Scatologia.

As stated above, the diagnosis was initially designed for individuals who make obscene phone calls. However, the legalized advent of calling a 900 number to make and receive an obscene phone call has significantly increased the number of individuals afflicted with this paraphilia. The incidence of telephone prostitution is virtually impossible to estimate because not all 900 numbers are related to phone sex. Fortunetellers and mystics also ply their trade on these phone lines. It is safe to say, however, that the quantity of 900 numbers directly related to phone sex is staggering.

These legal "pay for service" phone systems have brought the timid paraphiliac out of the closet. Men afflicted with Telephone Scatologia utilize obscene phone calls to strangers to achieve sexual arousal and orgasm. They may be incapable of developing and maintaining a social relationship—heterosexual or homosexual—that leads to sexual engagement. Some men utilize the legal phone sex services to fantasize sexual activity that their spouses or significant others find repugnant and, consequently, refuse to accommodate. Men whose partners refuse to accommodate their desire for oral or anal sex, for example, may turn to the phone for a descriptive conversation that they find intensely sexually arousing. They masturbate as they hear the description of the activity played out on the other end of the phone line. Men who are too timid to approach a prostitute on the street find the anonymity of phone sex especially appealing. They do not have to worry about the awkwardness of talking to a prostitute face to face or bargaining for sexual activity.

Commonly, a 900 phone number can be found in a pornographic magazine or catalogue with a picture of a gorgeous, scantily dressed or partially nude woman aligned with the telephone number. As the man dials the phone number and engages in conversation with the woman on the phone, he is looking at the photo, holding the phone in one hand and masturbating with the other. As disgusting as it may seem, this is a reality for thousands of men every day.

This technology has increased the number of men participating in Telephone Scatologia. What begins as a secretive, anonymous adventure into the sordid world of virtual prostitution often turns into a sexual paraphilia, one with serious implications. The only disadvantage of the activity for the caller is the charge for the phone call. The women on the opposite end of the line are carefully trained to keep the caller on the phone for as long as possible. A percentage of each call is profit for the owner of the line, so the longer the caller remains on the line, the greater the profit. The woman seductively holds the caller's attention. When the caller achieves orgasm, he hangs up the phone, thereby stopping the profit. The modus operandi of the 900 phone number is simple: Say whatever you need to say to keep the caller on the line without losing his sexual arousal. The caller is in phone-sex heaven. The woman verbally massages him to heightened sexual arousal and holds him there until his orgasm is maximized. Both parties appreciate the careful verbal manipulation. The longer the phone call, the greater the aggregate profit. The longer the subject is aroused, the more powerful the orgasm. A mutual satisfaction is achieved.

The heightened arousal and powerful orgasm are addictive and the caller becomes obsessed with making the next call. Further, the caller continues to fantasize regarding his relationship with this woman. The woman encourages this fantasy by telling the caller that his call was personally meaningful and produced her own sexual arousal. She informs him that all of the other callers are just "business as usual" and it is only his voice that sexually arouses her. This caller has been reeled in. He will call repeatedly, asking only for this woman. Numerous women operate the phone line and it is their objective to have him talk to someone other than the first woman. After hearing from another woman that she has "heard about what a wonderful caller he was" from the first woman, and that "she hopes she will have the opportunity to meet him and enjoy his company" as much as the first woman, he is caught again. She masterfully utilizes seductive descriptions to enhance his sexual arousal and bring him to orgasm.

This phone paraphilia comes crashing down when the caller receives his credit card bill and cannot pay it. Credit card companies make usury-like profits by extending the line of credit, increasing the percentage of interest charged on the balance, and permitting small monthly payments. Consequently, by the time the credit card company(s) rejects his credit card calls, he has already amassed an enormous debt. Further, by this time the Telephone Scatologia has become more severe, so the caller's need for stimulation via the phone call intensifies. The afflicted individual then turns to the illegal form of obscene phone calls, only to be arrested on a federal offense shortly thereafter.

As Internet technology increases and the cost for video observation decreases, the number of men afflicted with Telephone Scatologia will increase. Future editions of the DSM will probably identify a sexual paraphilia known as Internet Scatologia or something similar, where a caller can see his fantasy lover on his computer monitor as she talks to him. Careful to stay within the boundaries of FCC regulations, these women will keep callers on the phone even longer, increasing the profit accordingly. Thousands of men have reached financial disaster without the camera availability, and an even greater number will experience the same when they are able to view the woman on the other end of the phone line.

NECROPHILIA

Scenario

It has been a long day at the funeral home and the family of the deceased anxiously awaits the end of the day's visitation. The visitation time expires and the family departs. No one notices a man in his mid-20s sitting in the lobby. There are numerous visitations at this large funeral home.

Shortly after the family leaves, the man enters the visiting room and closes the door behind him. He approaches the casket and begins to fondle the breasts and genitalia of the elderly deceased woman. He becomes intensely sexually aroused and begins to unbutton her blouse. Fearful that he will be detected, he quickly raises her skirt as high as possible and takes a photo with his digital camera. He buttons her blouse, straightens her skirt, and quietly exits. He reassumes his position in the lobby awaiting the next family of a deceased person to leave. He contemplates asking the funeral home director if they are hiring employees.

This young adult has a sexual fixation with corpses. He is afflicted with *Necrophilia*.

Necrophilia Explained

One of the more bizarre sexual paraphilias is Necrophilia. The focus of Necrophilia is corpses. An individual afflicted with Necrophilia has recurrent, intense sexual arousal involving corpses. The severity of the paraphilia is identifiable by the behavior of the paraphiliac. Some individuals are sexually aroused merely by the sight or image of a corpse. On the opposite end of the continuum are the individuals who engage in sexual activity with a corpse. Regardless, the behavior and subsequent intense sexual arousal are aberrant.

The etiology of the paraphilia is differential. There are no characteristics common to all necrophiliacs. Some of the etiology is based on co-morbid mental illness and some on the circumstances relevant to the particular individual. Some serial killers' behaviors demonstrated a recurrent, intense sexual arousal with corpses. Jeffrey Dahmer, convicted of murdering numerous young men, admitted to committing sodomy with some of the corpses. In interviews with Dahmer, he admitted that he was obsessed with the goal of finding the most beautiful young man to be his "slave lover" for life. Dahmer, while admitting to sexual engagement with the corpses, surgically removed and preserved body parts, and he experimented with cannibalism as a means to keep his lovers with him always.

John Wayne Gacy was convicted of killing many adolescent males and burying them in the crawl space under his suburban Chicago home. Gacy was previously employed at a mortuary in Las Vegas, from which he was discharged for inappropriate activity with the corpses. Allegedly, Gacy was found inside a casket, coupled with a corpse.

Men who are unable to initiate and maintain age-appropriate sexual relationships regard themselves as sexually inadequate. Examples abound of the implications of an individual who perceives himself as sexually inadequate, but the most glaring and bizarre is Necrophilia. Due to the inability to develop a loving, sexual relationship with another person, regardless of age or gender, the person afflicted with Necrophilia resorts to sexual relationships with corpses.

PARTIALISM

Scenario

A strikingly attractive and athletically built young woman enters the jewelry store. The male clerks acknowledge her appearance with cautious glances while one clerk boldly approaches and asks if he can be of assistance. The young woman indicates that she is interested in a diamond ankle bracelet. The clerk directs her to the case displaying the bracelets. She picks out several to examine and then requests to try them on. The other male sales clerks watch with envy as she sits and raises her leg to try on the bracelets. The clerk discourages her and continues to hold her hand displaying the bracelets against her wrist. She prevails and he concedes. She personally puts the bracelets on her ankle to compare them. The sales clerk ignores her attractive legs and ankles. He stares at her hands and becomes sexually aroused.

This sales clerk is afflicted with the paraphilia *Partialism*. Touching a woman's hand intensely sexually arouses him. He sought the job at the jewelry store so he could admire hands, not ankles. If he was interested in ankles or feet he would have gone after a job at a shoe store.

Partialism Explained

A person afflicted with the sexual paraphilia Partialism exclusively focuses on a particular body part. The touching or mere observation or memory recall of the particular body part precipitates intense sexual arousal. Many men afflicted with this paraphilia develop an exclusive obsession with women's breasts, vaginas, buttocks, mouths, or thighs; some develop a focus on less obviously seductive body parts such as the feet, neck, or back. Homosexual males often develop Partialism for the penis and anus.

Most of these Partialism paraphiliacs begin their paraphiliac activity through the purchase of pornographic materials: magazines and videos.

Latex replications of breasts, vaginas, and anuses are available for purchase in pornography shops and through pornographic magazines. These paraphiliacs use these artificial body parts to masturbate while watching pornographic videos specific to the particular body part.

Partialism is commonly comorbid with other paraphilias. While these paraphiliacs do not commonly collect and preserve body parts, they often develop Fetishism for the garment that directly relates to the body part: panties, bras, shoes, and so forth. The Partialism is enhanced by the fetish, particularly if the item is soiled or used and maintains the characteristic scent of its owner.

Partialism is also commonly comorbid with legitimate and illegitimate Frotteurism. Legitimate Frotteurism would be individuals who are employed in a capacity that requires them to touch the specific body part(s) that relates to their paraphiliac focus. For example, an individual who has Partialism for feet may very well take a job as a shoe store clerk. In this capacity, he would be able to admire the focus of his sexual paraphilia. Partialism would very likely be comorbid with a shoe fetish and it would be appropriate for this person to touch the feet of his customers. Further, by straddling the foot bench, he can position his genitals in close proximity with the customer's foot. By raising the woman's foot as he puts on the shoe, he can also close his legs together, squeezing and stimulating his genitals. He can then place the foot back down on top of his closed thighs while he adjusts the shoe or ties the laces. If the individual is careful and not bold, he can repeat the same stimulation hundreds of times in a given day without disturbing a single customer. Many female shoppers are truly appreciative of the apparent extra attention they receive from the clerk. It is also a successful sales technique, as the woman will probably return to this store in the future and request service from the same clerk.

Gay men may solicit work in custom tailor stores. Men's custom slacks are cut to the exact length of the customer's inseam. Under the guise of an appropriate tailor's measurement, the paraphiliac can legitimately brush the inside of the customer's thigh and nudge his genitals.

Illegitimate Frotteurism comorbid with Partialism obviously includes the fondling of breasts and buttocks of nonconsenting people in crowded locations. What may appear as a case of Frotteurism may very well be Partialism with a focus on a particular body part. For example, a man may want only to touch breasts or some other sexually stimulating body part, and not to rub his genitals against the victim.

ZOOPHILIA

Scenario

John stops at the pet store on the way home from work to pick up "doggie treats" for his female golden retriever. Many people are gathered in front of the cages of the puppies, laughing at the antics of the young dogs playing with each other. John stops to watch the dogs at play and feels that familiar sensation in his groin. He is becoming sexually aroused. John quickly pays for the items and rushes home to engage in sexual activity with his dog.

John's aberrant sexual behavior is caused by *Zoophilia*.

Zoophilia Explained

Individuals afflicted with the sexual paraphilia Zoophilia experience recurrent, intense sexual arousal from behaviors and fantasies associated with animals.

Webster's Unabridged Dictionary (2001) defines bestial as "beastlike in gratifying one's sensual desires; carnal, debased" (p. 199) and bestiality as "brutish or beastly character or behavior" (p. 199). Bestiality should not be confused with Zoophilia.

An individual who engages in sexual intercourse with an animal is not practicing bestiality. He is committing sodomy with an animal. Further, the word sodomy is used to describe anal intercourse between two men.

Traditional definitions do not come close to describing the aberrant behavior that men and women engage in with animals. It is also very difficult to make a determination of the sexual paraphilia Zoophilia. The diagnosis requires that the individual experience recurrent, intense sexual arousal that has animals as its focus.

Consider the following dichotomy. The actual diagnosis is extremely rare, but aberrant sexual activity utilizing animals is much greater in incidence. Sexual engagement with animals is and has been the subject of pornography for decades and the aberrant activity appears to be increasing in incidence and diversity. It is vividly demonstrated on pornographic videos and on Internet Web sites. Whether an individual has recurrent, intense arousal pertaining to sexual activity with an animal is the relevant question. It is highly unlikely that this behavior is pathological, and it is more than likely either an adventurous behavior suggested by pornography or a commercial gimmick to sell pornography.

The incidence of a valid diagnosis of Zoophilia is extremely low and those individuals who are accurately diagnosed with this paraphilia are extremely disturbed. Men who are diagnosed with Zoophilia are not only incapable of developing an intimate relationship with an age-appropriate partner, they are also incapable of developing a sexual relationship with humans, and consequently have turned to animals for sexual fulfillment.

The American Psychiatric Association in the DSM-IV-TR (2000) indicates that with the exception of Sexual Masochism, sexual paraphilias are exclusively male (p. 568). To reiterate a previous point, it is not that women do not possess sexual paraphilias, but rather that the incidence of women compared to men is statistically so insignificant that it is not relevant to discuss women as sexual paraphiliacs. While the numbers of women who are clinically diagnosed with sexual paraphilias are few, certain paraphiliac-like behaviors in which they engage are instrumental in the development of paraphilias in others.

The aberrant behavior of a woman engaging in sexual intercourse with a German Shepherd dog or a Shetland pony may not be Zoophilia because she does not experience recurrent, intense sexual arousal from this behavior. Rather, she engages in this perverse sexual activity for monetary compensation. Explicit pornographic pictures or videos of women engaged in a variety of diverse aberrant sexual behaviors is sexually stimulating to the person observing it, not necessarily to the person performing the act. If a viewer becomes intensely sexually aroused by a woman's sexual engagement with animals, a diagnosis of Zoophilia is appropriate. Individuals who purchase videos and pictures of these sexual activities with animals, in contrast to pornography of a "human" nature, are zoophiliacs.

The diversity of sexual engagement with animals is beyond the creative imagination of nondysfunctional persons. Men and women have intercourse with a variety of mammals and perform oral sex on the male of the species. The practice of inserting animals—such as mice or snakes—into a woman's vagina is so commonplace that pornography shops and catalogues advertise products, such as funnels, to assist in the insertion process. There are many reported cases of hospital emergency room admissions in order to remove mice and snakes from the vaginas of women and the colons of both men and women. The animals could not be persuaded to exit, and consequently medical attention was required.

COPROPHILIA, UROPHILIA, KLISMAPHILIA

Coprophilia, Urophilia, Klismaphilia Explained

These three sexual paraphilias are discussed together because they all focus on human wastes eliminated by the body. Persons who have recurrent, intense sexual arousal pertaining to the wastes eliminated by the human body are generally diagnosed with one of the above-designated sexual paraphilias.

The focus of *Coprophilia* is human feces. Persons afflicted with Coprophilia experience recurrent, intense sexual arousal with the handling, eating, and association with human feces. It is most common for these individuals to be obsessed with a specific person. Their delusional fantasy of this person is so compulsive that they are sexually aroused by the thought of that person's feces. Coprophilia is commonly comorbid with other sexual paraphilia, but all of the paraphilias are focused on a particular individual. It is rare for an individual to be diagnosed with Coprophilia without a direct relationship with a particular person. The exceptions to this presumption pertain to people who are clinically impaired due to circumstances pertaining to toilet training. Individuals diagnosed with Coprophilia are commonly comorbid with Voyeurism, Partialism, and Fetishism.

Persons diagnosed with the sexual paraphilia *Urophilia* are focused on urine. The genitals that eliminate the urine arouse the disordered person. Heterosexual men diagnosed with Urophilia experience intense, sexual arousal when they consider the anatomical organ that eliminates the urine. It is not a fantasy of the kidney, but rather a fantasy regarding the vagina. It is not the urine that is sexually arousing, but rather the anatomical location from which it is emitted. Gay men are not interested in the urine itself but the penis that dispenses it.

Men afflicted with Urophilia ask their sexual partners for a "golden shower," requesting their partners, male or female, to urinate on them. This act is intensely sexually arousing to them.

The sexual paraphilia *Klismaphilia* has a focus of enemas. Normally considered a painful forceful elimination of wastes from the colon, persons afflicted with Klismaphilia experience intense sexual arousal from receiving an enema. This paraphilia is commonly comorbid with Sexual Masochism, as the pain associated with the filling of the colon with soapsuds or other liquid and restraining the elimination of the foreign liquid is often intense. The associated pain is sexually arousing to the paraphiliac and the final discharge is orgasmic in its physiological and psychological fulfillment.

Some clinicians contend that the forced cleansing of the colon has a guilt-redeeming value. Some gay men who practice sodomy with their partners continue to experience fear and guilt over their homosexuality and, specifically, anal intercourse. Enemas serve the dual purpose of cleansing the colon of the potentially contaminated semen of their sexual partner, while psychologically and spiritually cleansing their souls of the act of sodomy. The enema provides physiological cleansing of potentially AIDS-contaminated bodily fluid and spiritual cleansing of the soul for the sinful act.

Children raised in the 1940s, 1950s, and 1960s were subject to their mothers' paranoia regarding carcinogens in food additives. Additional research from Africa during that time suggested that due to a diet high in grains, which have a cathartic effect, the incidence of cancer in Africa was significantly lower than in developed countries. The aggregate effect of this research precipitated three behaviors in contemporary and educated mothers. They reduced their children's intake of animal products, they increased the intake of grains and other noncarcinogens that cleanse the colon, and they gave their children enemas to eliminate the potential cancerous products. Some mothers utilized castor oil to produce a laxative effect; however, some mothers preferred a soapy mixture enema to cleanse the potentially affected colon. Enemas produced a painful experience for the child, and the mother comforted the child while she inserted the enema tube. The holding and cuddling reinforced the child's ability to endure the painful enema and the desired result was achieved. Some of these children grew into adults who find sensual pleasure from the enema activity.

Although to many readers these paraphilias appear bizarre and far-fetched, they are real. However, their incidence is rare and likewise, so is sexual assault that demonstrates these paraphilias.

Chapter 5

Sexual Masochism, Sexual Sadism

Scenario

The gay and lesbian bar is filled to capacity and the band plays loud hard rock tunes. One attractive young man dressed in tight leather jeans and a silk top is surrounded by a group of men dressed in a more "macho" style of clothing. Sporting leather vests with chain adornments, these men offer the perfect view of uncovered arms with tattoos, and they are courting the attractive young man by displaying their dominance. After the demonstration of ritualized aggression, the young man makes his selection and the couple leaves the bar.

In the privacy of the macho male's apartment, the young attractive male begins to seductively strip for his chosen partner. Unwilling to wait, the partner pushes the young man down on the bed and roughly removes his silk shirt. The aggressive male eyes the silver nipple rings adorning the young man's chest and twists them, causing the young man to cry out in pain. The painful sensation is actually sexually stimulating to the young man. The aggressive male strips the leather pants from the young man and then flips him over on his stomach

His hands are handcuffed to the headboard. The aggressive male ties the young man spread eagle to the footboard. He removes his leather belt and strikes the young man across his buttocks. The aggressive male is sexually aroused by delivering the painful assault and the bound man is sexually aroused by receiving it. This giving and receiving of pain will be repeated a number of times throughout the night.

The young man is a *Sexual Masochist* who cannot achieve sexual arousal and orgasm in the absence of pain. His partner is a *Sexual Sadist* who cannot achieve sexual arousal and orgasm without delivering pain to his partner. They are consensual partners, each requiring the other to be sexually satisfied.

Sexual Masochism, Sexual Sadism Explained

Sexual Masochism and Sexual Sadism are discussed together because masochism and sadism are commonly comorbid. However, when the primary paraphilia is Sexual Masochism, the individual may exhibit characteristics of sadism as part of the sexual engagement. The individual with a primary paraphilia of Sexual Sadism is not particularly interested in masochistic behaviors and only permits them on a limited basis in comparison to the painful, suffering behaviors he delivers. The two paraphilias, however, require each other to achieve the intense sexual arousal the parties desire. While the characteristics are diametrically opposed, their cohabitation is requisite. Consequently, any discussion of Sexual Masochism must also include a discussion of Sexual Sadism.

Sexual Masochism Defined

"The paraphiliac focus of Sexual Masochism involves the act (real, not simulated) of being humiliated, beaten, bound, or otherwise made to suffer" (DSM-IV-TR, 2000, p. 572). A diagnosis of Sexual Masochism, similar to the other sexual paraphilias, requires that the behavior, sexual urges, or fantasies cause clinically significant distress or impairment in social, occupational, or other important areas of functioning (p. 566).

Sexual Masochism progresses in the severity of what is necessary to achieve arousal and orgasm. In the absence of the masochistic behavior, sexual arousal may not occur. Sexual Masochism is the only sexual paraphilia that is not considered male exclusive. A sufficient number of women are diagnosed with Sexual Masochism to attain statistical significance.

The question of reporting must be considered. Women who are diagnosed as Sexual Masochists are reported predominately by law enforcement agencies and hospital emergency room admissions. Self-reporting or family reporting of Sexual Masochism is limited to self-induced mutilation, body piercing, or oxygen deprivation. These particular behaviors may not be directly related to Sexual Masochism but, rather, could be behaviors associated with other social dysfunctional behavior or mental health conditions. Cutting, scarring, or other demonstrations of self-mutilations are not necessarily indicative of Sexual Masochism. Such mutilations may be attributed to other socially acceptable, as well as unacceptable, activities. Tattoos are acceptable, if not desirable, within certain social environments and they are commonplace within incarcerated populations. Young women experiencing bouts of depression mutilate themselves for reasons other than sexual stimulation.

Likewise, body piercing is not commonly considered a sexual paraphilia and is as commonplace as tattoos. Body piercing is usually done to attract attention from others. Women pierce their belly buttons to entice male attention, not because the activity is intensely sexually arousing. In contrast, some body piercing is part of the sexual activity of Sexual Masochists. Men and women pierce their nipples as part of sexual masochistic engagement.

The salient question regarding a particular painful activity is, Does it stimulate sexual arousal? Is being spanked during a sexual encounter an arousal behavior and does the recipient of the spanking want it? Masochism-afflicted males frequent prostitutes to pay them to perform painful behaviors on their bodies that their regular sexual partners are unwilling to do. Masochistic behaviors are diverse and may be comorbid with other paraphilias. Some individuals with Sexual Masochism are also afflicted with Klismaphilia. The intestinal cramping associated with an enema may be a sexually arousing stimulus. In this particular situation, the comorbidity of the two paraphilias may be self-induced, but in most circumstances Sexual Masochism is enhanced with a consenting sexual partner. Consequently, in the absence of a consenting sexual partner, individuals seek out prostitutes who are more than willing to deliver a painful sexual experience to their client.

A discussion of Sexual Masochism is incomplete without a thorough analysis of the paraphilia Sexual Sadism. While Sexual Masochism does exist independent of other paraphilias, the masochist is in constant search for a consenting partner to perform the painful acts. The individual afflicted with the paraphilia Sexual Sadism is not only willing to perform the desired painful activity, he also finds it intensely sexually arousing. In the eyes of the both sexual sadist and the sexual masochist, they have found the ideal partner. However, it is rare that the degrees of the severity of the paraphilias of the two individuals match, and it is at this point that the relationship turns from one of mutual acceptance to one of nonconsensual assault.

Sexual Sadism Defined

The paraphiliac focus of Sexual Sadism involves acts (real, not simulated) in which the individual derives sexual excitement from the psychological or physical suffering (including humiliation) of their victim. . . . In all of these cases, it is the suffering of the victim that is sexually arousing. Sadistic fantasies or acts may involve activities that indicate the dominance of the person over the victim (e.g., forcing the victim to crawl or keeping him in a cage). They may also involve restraint, blindfolding, paddling, spanking, whipping, pinching, beating, burning, electrical shocks, rape, cutting, stabbing, strangulation, torture, mutilation, or killing. (DSM-IV-TR, p. 573)

This DSM definition is one of the most important cited in this book. The majority of all lust homicides committed by serial killers demonstrates one or more of these characteristics. The sexual arousal and subsequent gratification of the behaviors inflicted upon victims is the driving motivation. The DSM-IV-TR continues its description with: "Sexual Sadism is usually chronic. . . . Usually, however, the severity of the sadistic acts increases over time. When Sexual Sadism is severe, and especially when it is associated with Antisocial Personality Disorder, individuals with Sexual Sadism may seriously injure or kill their victims" (p. 574).

The comorbid relationship of Sexual Sadism and Antisocial Personality Disorder will be discussed in depth in subsequent chapters. Sexual Sadism often exists as an independent paraphilia, but the behaviors associated with it are also characteristic of other paraphilias.

The most significant characteristic of Sexual Sadism is that it cannot be acted upon without a victim. Self-stimulation is not a characteristic of it, as it can be in most of the other paraphilias. The sexual sadist will utilize pornography to fantasize and stimulate, but that is merely temporary; the sadist requires the stimulation of personally inducing pain on a victim to achieve sexual arousal. The sexual sadist may be heterosexual, homosexual, or bisexual. He may prefer young, middle aged, or elderly victims. It is the pain and suffering of his victim that motivates him, not necessarily the characteristics of the victim. The pornographic material he utilizes in the absence of a "live" victim demonstrates his gender and age preference, but in reality, any encounter and engagement will suffice. He is not acting on displaced aggression to a particular gender, age group, race, or ethnic group. He is acting on the recurrent, intense sexual arousal that he achieves from producing physical or emotional suffering.

The true sexual sadist is an equal opportunity predator.

The sexual sadist preys on either consenting sexual masochists, prostitutes who are willing to endure his sadistic behavior, and/or nonconsenting victims. He will initially seek a consenting partner of the gender, age, and race that matches his fantasy lover. If that fantasy lover cannot be located, he is willing to accept any other consenting person. If no consensual partner can be located, he hires a prostitute. In the absence of a willing prostitute or sufficient money, he might seek out a weak, nonconsenting person.

The severity of the sadistic behavior is contingent on the type of partner the sadist locates. If he is successful in locating a consensual partner who meets his fantasy expectations, his sadistic behavior may be controlled by the willingness of his partner. Concerned about losing his consensual partner, he may reduce his sadistic demands to match the masochistic desires of his partner. He may restrain himself rather than risk the loss of the partner. However, he will require increasing levels of sadism to reach sexual arousal and will encourage his partner to participate. If his partner fails to comply with his wishes, he may well force the undesired behavior on his partner. The sexual sadist needs to produce pain and suffering, and he believes that once his partner experiences the new behavior, she or he will also be satisfied. In the absence of remorse, as with Sexual Sadism comorbid with an Antisocial Personality Disorder, the perpetrator will seek intensified sexual arousal, which in turn reinforces the forced behavior.

Once the sexual sadist tastes the pleasure of forcing pain, suffering, and humiliation beyond the wishes of the previously consenting partner, the search for consensual relationships decreases, and the search for heightened levels of stimulation increases. The sexual sadist may also reject his current lover as insufficiently adventurous and search for a new partner with similar tastes in behavior. Sadomasochistic relationships are dynamic, meaning ever-changing.

While Sexual Masochism and Sexual Sadism may exist in a comorbid state in an individual, it is more common for these two paraphilias to not be comorbid. One of the two sexual paraphilias is dominant. Consequently, one individual is predominately or exclusively a sexual sadist and the partner is predominately or exclusively a sexual masochist. Further, it is ludicrous to assume that two people possessing these opposite sexual paraphilias are in perfect sexual alignment with each other. Most commonly, the sexual sadist is more desirous of increased sadistic behaviors than the sexual masochist is interested in receiving or willing to endure. Conflict is inevitable. The masochist sets limits and the sadist does not. The two may explore increasingly higher levels of stimulating behavior, but eventually the masochist will draw the line beyond which more intense pain is unbearable and no longer sexually arousing. The two will not proceed beyond this particular level, which, while comfortable for the masochist, will eventually frustrate the sadist.

The stalemate is broken by the sadist, who searches for a more adventurous collaborator or forces the prohibited behavior on his current partner. This force is sexual assault.

Chapter 6

Transvestic Fetishism, Gender Identity Disorder

TRANSVESTIC FETISHISM

Scenario

Standing in front of the full-length mirror, the heterosexual male admires his female attire. He is not particularly attractive when dressed in gender-appropriate clothing, but he perceives himself as beautiful when fully adorned in women's clothing, a wig, and make-up. His effeminate stature is obvious when he wears men's clothing, but his femininity is enhanced in women's clothing. He will attract the admiring views of men and women tonight as he enters the transvestite culture. While his sexual preference is predominately heterosexual, he may be enticed into an occasional homosexual act. He is sexually stimulated by the vision of himself in all of his sensual femininity.

During the workday he must dress in men's clothing for outward appearances, but he secretly wears women's silk panties so that he can still enjoy his femininity. This heterosexual male is afflicted with *Transvestic Fetishism*.

GENDER IDENTITY DISORDER

Scenario

The couple emerges from the tavern. Slender and attractive, she is wearing a short skirt to show off her well-proportioned long legs. He is the picture of masculinity. Dressed in a Harley Davidson T-shirt, denim jacket, and leather motorcycle chaps, he is the epitome of macho. His hair is trimmed short on the sides of his head, with a perfect flattop and a pony-tail. As they approach the Harley "chopped hog," he squeezes her buttocks and kisses her. The lesbian couple mounts the motorcycle and drives off.

Disgusted with her biologically assigned gender, the woman dressed as a man is afflicted with *Gender Identity Disorder*.

Transvestic Fetishism Explained

The objective of this chapter is to simplify a complex discussion about heterosexual males who demonstrate the diagnostic criteria for the sexual paraphilia Transvestic Fetishism, and about both men and women who demonstrate the diagnostic criteria of Gender Identity Disorder. It is complex because Transvestic Fetishism is virtually exclusive to heterosexual males, but the demonstrative behaviors are very similar to males with Gender Identity Disorder, who may be heterosexual, homosexual, or bisexual in preference. Gender Identity Disorder is not exclusively a male disorder, and consequently, the sexual preference of women with the disorder further complicates the discussion. No clean lines of distinction exist; instead, gender preference, identity disorder, and sexual paraphilia blend together to produce behavioral manifestations that defy diagnosis.

An individual who cross-dresses may truly be suffering from Gender Identity Disorder. He may abhor his genitals and wish they were cut off. Or he may have Transvestic Fetishism and simply become sexually aroused by wearing women's clothing.

Transvestic Fetishism Defined

"The paraphiliac focus of Transvestic Fetishism involves cross-dressing by a male in women's attire" (p. 574). Note that this definition does not include women who dress in men's clothing. Consequently, the American Psychiatric Association has described this sexual paraphilia as male exclusive.

Because Transvestic Fetishism, as all sexual paraphilias, must meet the generic diagnostic requirements, the following list is for review.

1. Recurrent, intense sexual arousal
2. Clinically significant distress or impairment in social, occupational, or other important areas of functioning

3. Violations of law in some cases

4. Specific requirements for arousal

Before getting into further description of the behavioral manifestations of this sexual paraphilia, it is critical to acknowledge the following criteria from the DSM-IV-TR: "This disorder has been described only in heterosexual males" (p. 574). This one sentence is definitive. Gay men who wear women's clothing are *not* afflicted with Transvestic Fetishism. Only heterosexual males who become intensely sexually aroused by cross-dressing can be accurately diagnosed with Transvestic Fetishism. Gay men who cross-dress with the motivation of locating a consensual homosexual partner are not diagnosed with Transvestic Fetishism. "Transvestic Fetishism is NOT diagnosed when cross-dressing occurs exclusively during the course of Gender Identity Disorder" (p. 574). It is important to recognize and understand the significance of this difference.

Cross-dressing is not just limited to individuals who are afflicted with Transvestic Fetishism or Gender Identity Disorder, but is also an active, relevant behavior of men and women who have a nontraditional gender preference. Men who choose men as life and/or sexual partners may choose to cross-dress as part of the relationship. The film *The Birdcage* is an example of two males who live in a domestic relationship in which one chooses to dress in traditional female clothing and the other chooses to dress in traditional male clothing. Are either of these characters portraying a sexual paraphilia or Gender Identity Disorder? The answer is *no*. Examination of Gender Identity Disorder, described later in this chapter, demonstrates that the diagnostic criteria for neither it nor Transvestic Fetishism have been met. This is a challenge to our philosophical position on "inclusiveness." What, if any, dysfunction exists? Is the couple dysfunctional?

The DSM-IV-TR statement complicates the diagnosis of Transvestic Fetishism even more with, "although his basic preference is heterosexual, he tends to have few [heterosexual (comment added)] sexual partners and may have engaged in occasional homosexual acts" (p. 574). In summation, a heterosexual male afflicted with Transvestic Fetishism has recurrent, intense sexual arousal from wearing women's apparel, has few sexual encounters, and may have engaged in homosexual activity.

The behavioral range of the paraphilia also demonstrates the severity of the disorder. Some men may choose to wear only one item of women's apparel under their otherwise traditional male clothing, while other men cross-dress completely, including make-up and feminine hairstyles. Some men engage in the paraphiliac activity occasionally, while other men become deeply engrossed in a transvestic subculture.

As we move our discussion to Gender Identity Disorder, it is important to reemphasize that Transvestic Fetishism is a sexual paraphilia in which dressing in women's garments is the focus of the intense sexual arousal, not any subsequent sexual engagement. While the individual may become aroused during sexual engagement, Transvestic Fetishism produces intense arousal independently. Most activity of men afflicted with Transvestic Fetishism is self-erotic, with masturbation being the orgasmic mechanism.

Gender Identity Disorder Defined

Gender Identity Disorder is *not* a sexual paraphilia, but it is discussed here because of the similarity in behavioral manifestation with Transvestic Fetishism. The DSM-IV-TR defines Gender Identity Disorder as follows:

There are two components of Gender Identity Disorder, both of which must be present to make the diagnosis. There must be evidence of a strong and persistent cross-gender identification, which is the desire to be, or the insistence that one is, of the other sex (Criterion A). The cross-gender identification must not merely be a desire for any perceived cultural advantages of being the other sex. There must also be evidence of persistent discomfort about one's assigned sex or a sense of inappropriateness in the gender role of that sex. (p. 576)

Gender Identity Disorder Explained

The onset of Gender Identity Disorder may be at a very young prepubescent age in both boys and girls. Young boys who prefer to wear girls' clothing, play with traditionally girls' toys, engage in girls' activities, and forge peer relationships with girls may be experiencing Gender Identity Disorder. If the same boy rejects the "roughhousing" activities common to young boys, such as contact athletics and male-associated toys, the rejection lends further credibility to such a diagnosis. If the boy demonstrates disgust for his penis and indicates that he does not want it or wishes that he had a vagina, the diagnosis is generally confirmed.

Girls who want to wear boys' clothing, wear their hair in a boyish cut, and reject commonly considered feminine activities might be diagnosed with Gender Identity Disorder. The diagnosis may be further confirmed if the young girl prefers male peers over female, engages in roughhousing common to young boys, and overtly rejects girls' toys and play in favor of boys' toys and play. Finally, the diagnosis is confirmed if the young girl indicates a desire to grow a penis and refuses to urinate sitting down.

Preadolescent Gender Identity Disorder is challenged at the time of enrollment into elementary school. While clinical referrals are common at this time, it is also when the disorder begins to dissipate, particularly in boys. Young boys who grow up in a female-dominated family adopt behaviors that are modeled on their sisters and other female relatives. A young boy who is raised in a family headed by a single mother and who only has female siblings may adopt these superficial Gender Identity Disorder behaviors for acceptance. Typically, these behaviors are maternally reinforced.

Bandura (1977), a developmental psychologist, suggests that children learn through emulation and by observing behaviors in others. Consequently, the young man raised in a female-dominant family may develop female interests and female mechanisms for problem solving. With respect to relationships with males, the young boy can develop not only feminine skills for handling social problems, but also a gender-biased attitude regarding males. Likewise, a young girl raised in a family dominated by males can learn that roughhousing is a means of self-protection, and that the behavior is rewarded by the dominant male figure of the household. The young girl can also learn to compete very successfully in male-dominated sports. Further, fathers intent on developing masculine traits in their sons are more apt to use disparaging comments with their sons than their daughters, for example, "You run like an old woman" or "Your sister just whooped you, boy."

Familial situations like the ones described above generally dissipate as children enroll in school. Upon hearing disparaging comments from schoolmates, the majority of the boys change their behavior to model traditional gender roles. Girls, in contrast, become more competitive, informing the world that they are as tough and athletic as their brothers and the "wimps" at school. Consequently, tomboys can excel and become gender and sports "heroes." Conversely, boys who have been raised in female-dominated environments have two choices : reject their female influence or adopt it as a way of life.

> Females with Gender Identity Disorders generally experience less ostracism because of cross-gender interests and may suffer less from peer rejection, at least until adolescence. In child clinic samples, boys with this disorder are referred for evaluation much more frequently than are girls. In adult clinical samples, men outnumber women by about two or three times. In children, the referral bias toward males may partly reflect the greater stigma that cross-gender behavior carries for boys than girls. (DSM-IV-TR, 2000, p. 579)

Only a small number of children who demonstrate behaviors characteristic of Gender Identity Disorder carry the disorder into adulthood. Of those that do, nearly 75 percent of the males report they have a gay or bisexual orientation without the associated Gender Identity Disorder. The majority of the remaining males report either a heterosexual orientation or, in the most severe cases, a continuation of Gender Identity Disorder. Some may seek sex reassignment surgery. Further, some of those males who report a heterosexual orientation without Gender Identity Disorder are afflicted with Transvestic Fetishism.

The variety of alternatives often perplexes clinicians and, consequently, nonclinically educated persons are at a loss to understand the behavior. It is considered aberrant to individuals who possess traditional sexual orientations. Our focus is on sexual predators, so it is therefore necessary to inquire if Transvestic Fetishism or Gender Identity Disorder is significant to the study of sexual predators. While this paraphilia and disorder are not considered indicators of sexual predators, the circumstances change significantly when they exist in a comorbid state with other paraphilias and personality disorders.

Chapter 7

Pedophilia, Hebephilia

PEDOPHILIA

Scenario

The preschool and elementary children are playing in the "children only" area of the fast food center of the indoor mall. Their mothers are enjoying the peace and quiet, the opportunity to have an adult conversation over their lunch. They feel secure in their knowledge that a security guard is watching over their children.

The mall security guard carefully watches the activities of the children. His close observation locates a beautiful 6-year-old blond girl with pigtails. She looks just like the little girl wearing the pajamas in the Penney's catalog. He watches intently and feels that familiar sensation in his groin as his penis enlarges to full erection. With the assistance of a jock strap and very baggy pants, his physical sexual arousal goes undetected. He sits down, puts his hands in his pockets, and strokes his penis. He wishes he had a camera, but photographing the child would be too obvious.

As the young girl responds to her mother's call that it is time to go home, the guard calls the mall security office on his radio to inform them he is taking his break. As the mother and child depart for the parking garage, the security officer follows them at a discreet distance and records the license number of the family's vehicle. Upon returning to the mall office, he calls the DMV to report a suspicious looking vehicle in the parking garage. The DMV clerk, too busy to follow protocol, gives the mall security officer the name and address of the person who owns the vehicle.

This mall security officer suffers from *Pedophilia*. He is sexually aroused over this little girl and has masterfully identified her residence.

HEBEPHILIA

Scenario

Disneyland is Disneyland. The warm, dry weather has brought out families in droves. Mothers, fathers, children of all ages, and grandparents as well, flock to the amusement park in anticipation of a day full of excitement.

Standing alone, a man watches the crowds of people flow back and forth to their favorite attractions. As a family walks by, the mid-30s mother draws the attention of male observers. Wearing extremely short shorts, high heel sandals, and a halter top too skimpy to hold her ample breasts, she parades through the park watching her children enjoy the rides. The man ignores the mother as her 13-year-old daughter wearing shorts and a T-shirt catches his eye.

He stares intently at the pubescent girl and decides to follow the family. This man has no interest in the skimpily clad mother. He is sexually aroused by the visions of this virginal-appearing pubescent girl. This man suffers from *Hebephilia*.

Pedophilia, Hebephilia Explained

The DSM-IV-TR does not differentiate between Pedophilia and Hebephilia. It only designates the Sexual Paraphilia of Pedophilia. "The paraphiliac focus of Pedophilia involves sexual activity with a prepubescent child (generally age 13 years or younger)" (p. 571). While a classification of Hebephilia does not appear in the DSM, a distinction in victim characteristics is of significant importance to law enforcement, schools, and child social servicing agencies.

The paraphiliac focus of Hebephilia involves sexual activity with pubescent and post-pubescent children, those in middle school or junior high school. The primary difference in the diagnostic criteria of Hebephilia and Pedophilia is the age of the victim; consequently, the two will be discussed concurrently throughout this chapter, acknowledging the differences that may appear due the age of the victims.

The following generic sexual paraphiliac qualifiers apply to both Pedophilia and Hebephilia:

1. Recurrent, intense sexual arousal
2. Clinically significant distress or impairment in social, occupational, or other important areas of functioning
3. Violations of law in some cases
4. Specific requirements for arousal

One DSM diagnostic criterion is *not* a qualifier for Pedophilia and Hebephilia:

> It is important to understand that experiencing distress about having the fantasies, urges or behaviors is *not* necessary for a diagnosis of Pedophilia. Individuals who have a pedophiliac arousal pattern and act on these fantasies or urges with a child qualify for the diagnosis of Pedophilia. (p. 571)

Persons afflicted with other paraphilias, as previously discussed, experience distress while the pedophile does not. Distress may take the form of great pain, sorrow, anxiety, or trouble with social relationships. Many individuals suffering from paraphilias experience guilt over their overwhelming desire to commit behaviors that are considered socially unacceptable. Further, the intensely, arousing urges and fantasies commonly produce physiological arousal in the form of an erection, which may be observable through the person's clothing in public places. Even if the erection is not observable, the individual often perceives that it is and this perception produces distress. Men suffering from paraphilias may wear baggy clothing and coats. The public perception that sexually disordered men wear long overcoats or raincoats because they are naked underneath is accurate only in relationship to those exhibitionists who are actively stalking subjects. More commonly, paraphiliac men wear this clothing so that they can disguise their erections and self-stimulate in public without being detected. Paraphiliacs cut out the bottom of their coat pockets so that they can stimulate their penis with their hand without opening their coat or taking down the zipper, thus exposing themselves in public. This is of particular significance to men who are afflicted with Frotteurism and require the nonconsensual touching of others in public places. Following the nonconsensual touching, the paraphiliac can masturbate in relative obscurity, in public, while the memory of the touching is fresh.

Distress may also take the form of intense anxiety, which can occur in the process of the active behavioral manifestation of the paraphilia and in the absence of the fantasy object, fetish, or behavior. As an individual prepares to act on his paraphilia, he experiences intense anxiety related to anticipation and fear of being detected as he approaches the behavior. He experiences physiological symptoms of anxiety, including increased heart rate and heightened blood pressure, sweating, difficulty in swallowing, shallow breathing, dryness of the mouth, and, often, speech impairment. As the object of the paraphilia becomes closer, the symptoms increase and culminating behavior is disorganized and often appears chaotic. For example, when an individual suffering from Exhibitionism succumbs to the intense sexual urge and decides to leave the safety of his home and go out into the public to exhibit his genitalia, the anxiety begins. As he dresses in preparation for his venture, the fantasy of the encounter becomes more vivid and the anxiety increases. This anxiety continues to escalate as he leaves his house, travels to his predetermined location, and begins the visual stalk for the appropriate victim. The intensity becomes overwhelming as he identifies and approaches his victim. By the time he opens his coat to expose his penis, he is fully erect and may, without manual stimulation, ejaculate.

The paraphiliac experiences great anxiety also in the absence of his behavior. The paraphiliac uses pornography, masturbation, and, commonly, alcohol to subdue his recurring urges, fantasies, and desires. When he cannot act upon these intense sexual urges, he experiences anxiety. The anxiety is reduced temporarily by pornography and masturbation. It becomes necessary to utilize diversity in the pornography, alcohol, and drugs in order to achieve orgasm and relief from the recurring urges and associated anxiety. Eventually, the pornographic stimulation is insufficient to achieve orgasm and relief from the anxiety, and the individual takes his paraphilia into the public. It is at this time that the anxiety of anticipation and the fear of discovery and apprehension begin to overwhelm him.

Venturing into public without the intent of acting on the paraphilia is also very distressful for afflicted individuals. Visual and auditory stimuli are commonly present and the intense sexual arousal reoccurs. The simple act of grocery shopping can expose the individual to stimuli that will precipitate paraphiliac urges and the associated physical arousal. Individuals may not be able to maintain normal employment and social relationships. The sexual arousal may begin to preoccupy the individual's life, and he may make an employment change to accommodate his paraphilia.

The distress discussed above is characteristic of all of the paraphilias except Pedophilia and Hebephilia. *Pedophiles and hebephiles do not experience guilt associated with their socially unacceptable fantasies, urges, and behaviors. This lack of guilt and distress makes the pedophile and hebephile dangerous and serial in behavior.*

Legal Definitions of a Minor Child

Individuals imprisoned for criminal sexual misconduct with children may or may not be pedophiliac. The DSM-IV-TR provides some specific exclusion to the diagnostic criteria for Pedophilia. "The person is at least 16 years and at least five years older than the child or children in Criterion A (generally age 13 years or younger). . . . Note: Do not include an individual in late adolescence involved in an ongoing sexual relationship with a 12- or 13-year-old" (p. 572). State legislators do not necessarily follow the DSM diagnostic criteria in the promulgation of criminal statutes, and consequently many individuals are sentenced to prison as the result of sexual conduct with minor children.

The definition of minor children is not consistent from state to state. In some states, a child is considered a minor at age 16—an adolescent male of 17 years engaged in sexual conduct with a 16-year-old consenting female has committed criminal sexual conduct, historically referred to as statutory rape. The behavior is illegal because of the age ascribed to the female participant in the sexual activity, regardless of consent. States have determined that not until a person reaches a statutorily designated age can this person consent to sexual engagement; thus, the older, nonminor male has committed an act of criminal sex conduct. The 17-year-old male in this scenario may be charged, convicted, and imprisoned as a sex offender, a label that he will carry for the rest of his life.

The Articles of Federation persuaded the framers of the U.S. Constitution to allow individual states to govern their own citizens and write laws to prescribe socially acceptable behavior. Regional differences in conservatism and liberalism cause state legislators to promulgate statutes that reflect the opinion of their constituents. Therefore, differences exist among states pertaining to age of majority, age of consent to sexual engagement, and criminal sexual conduct. A 17-year-old male who engages in sexual activity with a 16-year-old girl may be considered a sexual offender in one state but not in an adjacent state. Persons imprisoned for sexual conduct in one state would not be prosecuted for the same behavior in another state. Therefore, it is important that the diagnosis of Pedophilia be carefully established in light of the DSM rather than state criminal codes. The following discussion does not pertain to individuals who are incarcerated for criminal sexual conduct with a consensual partner who is considered a minor child only by statute. Rather, it pertains to those individuals who have a valid diagnosis of Pedophilia.

DSM-IV-TR Diagnosed Pedophiles

Pedophiles who have been convicted and sentenced to prison for crimes of sexual misconduct against minor children indicate during interviews with clinicians and law enforcement personnel that they do not believe their love interests or behavior with children is abnormal and that they experience no anxiety regarding it. The lack of guilt or remorse is not precipitated by a deficiency in conscience or morality—the disordered person believes his love interests and subsequent behaviors with children are appropriate. They further indicate that they have no other age-appropriate love interests.

Much research and debate revolves around the etiology of Pedophilia. The DSM-IV-TR offers no information as to the origin of Pedophilia. The behavior in itself suggests that the pedophile is insecure with age-appropriate relationships and finds relationships with children less anxiety producing. It is generally acknowledged that the onset of Pedophilia coincides with puberty and adolescents even though most pedophiles do not act on their urges until later in life. Adolescents who have difficulty establishing mainstream relationships with age-appropriate peers turn to younger children for companionship. These adolescent-child relationships are not anxiety producing and, consequently, are reinforcing. The adolescent—socially inept with age-appropriate peers and fearful of ridicule and lack of social acceptance—continues his relationships with younger children.

The sexual experimentation of adolescence is anxiety producing to even the most mainstream youth and is overwhelming to the socially inept youth. Experimentation with younger children is easier and therefore rewarding. The pattern continues into adulthood. The adult pedophile, recalling pleasant, anxiety-free sexual relationships with children, finds little reason to alter his pattern. Attempts to counteract his pedophilia with sexual encounters with age-appropriate peers are commonly met with anxiety, frustration, and disillusionment. The failure to develop age-appropriate relationships reinforces two beliefs of the pedophile: age-appropriate relationships are unattainable, and sexual relationships with children are pleasurable, rewarding, attainable, and desirable. The pedophile becomes fixated on the delusion that somewhere there is a child that desires him as much as he desires him or her and therefore it is not only appropriate, but also vital to both parties.

Some researchers suggest that the origin of Pedophilia can be traced to childhood sexual experiences with significant adults. Parents, older siblings, and other relatives who sexually molest young children may influence the development of the disorder in the victim. If the sexual experience is associated with a display of love and affection, and the sexual interaction is not painful to the child, then the child will associate the sexual activity as relevant, appropriate, and desirable. Youths who have been identified as molesting younger children have invariably been molested themselves as children. They are not attempting to inflict pain on the younger child, but rather are demonstrating love and affection as it was demonstrated to them.

No single theory can explain the etiology of Pedophilia and Hebephilia. Instead, many variables may precipitate this disorder in psychosocial development.

The anxiety that pedophiles and hebephiles do experience is directly related to their inability to identify and attain a relationship with their fantasy lover. In order to reduce their levels of anxiety, they resort to pornography, alcohol, and masturbation. Unfortunately, these substitutes are short lived and eventually the pedophile finds it necessary to leave the privacy of his home to find his fantasy lover. Video representations no longer suffice and the individual requires the observation of the desired group of children.

Pedophiles are not intellectually deficient, and they are fully aware of the legal consequences of being caught in a relationship with a child. They believe the laws are discriminatory and the punishments severe. It is the fear of being caught, prosecuted, and sentenced to prison that deters their behavior outside the confines of their homes. The inability to attain the relationship and the fear of legal reprisal precipitates their anxiety. As the inability to locate and attain their ideal lover increases, so does the level of anxiety. It is when this level of heightened anxiety increases that the likelihood of illegal conduct multiplies.

The first excursions into illegal conduct take place within the relative safety of the pedophile's home. The purchase and possession of child pornography is illegal, and if apprehended with it in his possession, the pedophile will be subject to public prosecution and sentencing. It is not the fear of apprehension that is most anxiety producing to him, but rather the public exposure associated with prosecution. Newspaper accounts of the arrest, trial, and sentencing will put his face before the public and he will lose his anonymity. This will reduce his ability to move about the community and observe children in hopes of identifying his ideal fantasy lover.

Most states have passed laws that place convicted sex offenders on the equivalent of "watch" lists. These lists differ from the lists maintained by law enforcement agencies for wanted criminals or terrorists. These sex offender registration lists are readily available to the public via the Internet. Anyone can visit a state, city, or county sex offender list to view a picture of the offender and obtain his address and conviction record. These lists are delineated by neighborhoods or zip codes, allowing community members to identify neighbors who are convicted sex offenders. The laws also require that convicted sex offenders report changes in address. When a pedophile is apprehended and convicted for a sex-related crime with a minor child, his name, picture, and other vital characteristics are immediately posted to the Web site.

Commonly, this public exposure precipitates a physical move on the part of the offender. The convicted sex offender moves to a different neighborhood. If the offender is under the jurisdiction of a supervising probation or parole officer, he will require permission of the corrections officer to relocate and he must report his new address. The offender cannot leave the county or state without the permission of the officer. Failure to obtain permission for relocation is a violation of the conditions of his probation or parole and will result in a loss of his conditional freedom. Incarceration will ensue. However, if the offender is no longer under the continuing supervision of the Department of Corrections, he may change his residence—including city, county, and state—without permission.

The sex offender registration statute requires that the convicted sex offender report his new address to the local law enforcement agency in his new community. This is where the concept of sex offender registration loses effectiveness. The statutes dictate that the offender will report his location for the remainder of his life; however, in the absence of Department of Corrections supervision, control mechanisms for tracking the relocated offender are ineffective.

It is ludicrous to believe that a relocating sex offender will report his new residence to the local law enforcement agency of his own volition. The convicted sex offender cannot wait for the day that his supervision is terminated so that he can regain the freedom that has eluded him for the entire duration of his community supervision. It is a foregone conclusion: The convicted sex offender will move as soon as he is no longer under supervision and he will not report his new residence to the authorities. Consequently, he reestablishes his anonymity.

The disadvantages of reporting one's new residence are obvious to the pedophile. His name, picture, and conviction record are posted on the new community's Web site. His new neighbors locate his picture and particulars, and again, he is subject to public scrutiny and discrimination. There are numerous accounts of vigilante activity by community members to drive registered convicted sex offenders out of their neighborhoods. The offenders cannot leave their houses without suspicion and the neighbors establish a special neighborhood watch for him. His whereabouts are constantly reported to the local law enforcement officials, and he is an automatic suspect for all crime in the neighborhood.

In the case of the convicted pedophile, the lack of anonymity restricts his ability to move around the community observing groups of children. The pedophile also perceives this lack of mobility as his inability to identify and attain a relationship with his desired fantasy lover. His anxiety is exacerbated and the tendency to violate increases.

When a convicted sex offender is terminated from supervision, changes residence, and does not report his new residency, the new community is endangered. Not until he is stopped for a traffic violation or arrested on another charge is his identity as a convicted sex offender exposed, unless the community chooses to scrutinize strangers and their behaviors.

Therefore, it is a frightening time for the pedophile, when he no longer finds fulfillment in pornography and masturbation. Even his previous excursions to adult bookshops are anxiety producing. The U.S. Supreme Court has ruled on numerous occasions pertaining to the 1st Amendment right of freedom of the press and the subsequent availability of pornographic material. Visiting an adult bookstore and purchasing adult pornography are legal activities, but the production, selling, and possession of child pornography are illegal. Pedophiles must locate sources of illegal child pornographic material.

Owners of adult bookstores usually do not risk the apprehension, prosecution, store closure, and the loss of enormous profits by selling child pornography. It is common practice for law enforcement officers, working undercover, to pose as sellers and buyers of child pornography. The storeowner who purchases child pornography from an undercover officer faces prosecution, store closure, and a prison sentence. The storeowner who procures child pornography in the illicit market and sells it to an undercover officer faces the same. Consequently, child pornography is not available over the counter at adult bookstores.

Child pornography is available only through underground networks. Pedophiles do not tend to work in tandem with other pedophiles. While they certainly can identify other pedophiles by their behavior, they avoid each other. The pedophile is not interested in sharing his observation of a group of children, of which his fantasy lover may be a member. He is also sufficiently paranoid and would wonder if the other apparent pedophile is an undercover officer. For this reason, obtaining child pornographic material is difficult and anxiety producing for the neophyte or relocated pedophile. However, as in all marketplaces, if a buyer exists, a seller will appear.

Although child pornography sites do not exist on the Internet, adult pornography sites provide the conduits to child pornography. The neophyte or ignorant pedophile who attempts to procure child pornography from an Internet site can be discovered by law enforcement officials who monitor these Internet sites, their email addresses, and chat rooms.

Contacts for obtaining illegal pornography come from the street. Employees, not owners, of adult bookstores are knowledgeable on how to obtain all types of illegal pornography through the underground network. For a finder's fee, both from the buyer and the seller, these employees will bring the parties together. While it is obvious that this is the logical setting for a sting operation, the sheer number of adult bookstores makes the potential for successful intervention and deterrence impossible. The bookstore employees scrutinize their inquiring customers for the potential for undercover law enforcement.

Purveyors of child pornography are close to other illicit activities. Neighborhoods frequented by prostitutes and drug dealers are havens for the sellers of illegal pornography. They stand on the same corners and quietly inform potential customers of their wares. The street vice community is a closed and tight one. Outsiders other than customers are carefully scrutinized. Customers are scrutinized as well, as undercover officers come from both sides—the sellers and the buyers of vice products.

These initial excursions to find child pornography are anxiety producing for the pedophile, but the potential for a successful contact and the purchase of the desired material is overwhelmingly reinforcing. Once a source is located, the pedophile runs back to the obscurity of his home to pleasure himself. The pedophile will return to the same network to purchase more materials once the older pornography no longer produces his desired levels of satisfaction and gratification. If the Penney's or Sears catalogues provided sufficient pleasurable stimulation, then the initial foray into the world of child pornography would not be necessary. The pedophile ventures further out in the world when the combination of pornography, alcohol, drugs, and masturbation no longer satisfies him. The visual and audio stimulation lose their gratifying and arousal-achieving value, and the time arrives for the pedophile to look for alternative stimuli.

Most pedophiles are victim-age and -gender specific. The DSM-IV-TR indicates that:

> Individuals with Pedophilia generally report an attraction to children of a particular age range. Some individuals prefer males, others females; and both males and females arouse some. Those attracted to females usually prefer 8- to 10-year-olds, whereas those attracted to males usually prefer slightly older children. Pedophilia involving female victims is reported more often than pedophilia involving male victims. . . . the course is usually chronic, especially in those attracted to males. The recidivism rate for individuals with Pedophilia involving a preference for males is roughly twice that for those who prefer females. (p. 571)

Pedophiles will commonly visit children's clothing departments in large retail stores. Many fathers purchase clothing for their children, so the presence of a man in a children's clothing department is not considered abnormal or suspicious. Because the pedophile has identified his perfect fantasy lover who has a gender and an age, he will enter the clothing department relevant to the gender and age of this fantasy lover. He will locate and fondle underclothing and sleeping garments that would be appropriate for his lover. The pedophile will buy the clothing that is visually and tactually most stimulating to him. He will take the clothing to the privacy of his home and blend the new stimuli with the old. He will caress the clothing, rub it against his face, and stimulate his genitals with it. He will close his eyes and see his fantasy lover in the clothing, and he will imagine different scenarios with different articles of clothing. He will imagine different stages of undress as he masturbates.

While the garment appears to be a fetish, it is not the clothing that is sexually stimulating. It is the fantasy of the clothing as a possession of his fantasy lover that is sexually arousing. A diagnosis of Fetishism requires "recurrent, intense sexually arousing fantasies, sexual urges, or behaviors involving the use of nonliving objects" (DSM-IV-TR, 2000, p. 570). The DSM-IV-TR further indicates that "usually the fetish is required or strongly preferred for sexual excitement, and in its absence there may be erectile dysfunction in males" (p. 569). For pedophiles, the garment is not requisite for sexual arousal, but the image of the fantasy lover is.

Searches of the residences of pedophiles commonly reveal new garments for children. The practice of purchasing children's clothing is safe for the pedophile and temporarily excites him and provides a source of gratification. However, the need for heightened levels of stimulation eventually negates the value of the purchased clothing, which has a significant shortcoming: a child has not worn it.

The new clothing has a scent of new cloth and, after utilization as an erotic stimulator, the personal odor of the pedophile, not his fantasy lover. Laundered, it has the scent of detergent, bleach, and softener. As the value of the purchased clothing decreases, the anxiety level of the pedophile increases. The pedophile must identify new alternative stimuli.

The pedophile leaves his home to look at children. He intimately knows the characteristics of his fantasy lover and he goes into the world to locate him or her. Children are found everywhere, but the search will be delineated according to the gender and age of his fantasy lover. Some generic locations are generally safe from detection for a pedophile. Adults and children of all ages regularly visit parks, playgrounds, shopping malls, zoos, and amusement parks. A pedophile can take a seat on a park bench and, in relative obscurity, watch children. Many adults visit the park to eat their lunch, feed the pigeons, and "people watch." It is not a violation of the law. The pedophile can stroll around the park looking for a group of children of the appropriate age and gender. Upon locating a group of children of the relevant age and gender of his fantasy lover, he can find a place to sit and observe. Inclement weather will force parents, children, and pedophiles indoors to shopping malls, theaters, and enclosed coliseums. The pedophile adjusts his location accordingly.

The pedophile may be more direct in his attempt to find the perfect group to observe. If his fantasy lover is an eight-year-old boy, he might locate little league soccer games, age group swim meets, or Cub Scout activities. It is extremely significant to note that all pedophiles have a preferred fantasy lover and this preference is their first choice to locate and observe. The characteristics of the victim group assist in predicting the future whereabouts of a pedophile.

This observation of children is analogous to Voyeurism. The pedophile is conducting a nonconsenting visual search for his fantasy lover. He is carefully watching for the appearance of the child that most closely resembles his fantasy lover. The image may be very specific to a child he has found in the children's underwear section in a department store catalogue. He cuts out the pictures and keeps them preserved. The image may be from a child pornography magazine or video. On the other hand, it may be less specific and generic to many children of the correct race, age, and gender. Regardless, he will study the children as they play or pass by.

Once he finds a child that is representative of his child fantasy lover, he will record a visual memory of the child, take that memory back to the privacy of his home, and blend this real image with his other stimuli to excite and gratify him. If the desired child is found in a location specific to the child's interest, such as a soccer field or swimming pool, the pedophile will return to observe again. If others are photographing or videotaping the event, he will do likewise and take home a replay of the child's image that he can utilize at any time he is desirous of stimulation and gratification.

The pedophile who successfully locates his fantasy lover develops a delusion that the child loves him in return and anticipates their meeting and developing a relationship. This delusion alters the pedophile's course from searching for the perfect lover to planning how to meet this lover.

The pedophile may attempt to locate and take a personal item of the child. The soccer warm-up suit worn by the child and taken off before participation in the match is a treasure to the pedophile. Not only does he have a visual image—memory and/or photographic—he also has an item of the child's clothing that holds the child's scent. The pedophile adds this article of clothing to his growing cache of stimuli.

The creation of a plan to meet the child is a premeditated stalk. Stalking behavior is diverse and is contingent on numerous variables, including the mental health of the pedophile. Stalking patterns are discussed in Chapter 10.

As indicated in the beginning of this chapter, the diagnostic criteria for Pedophilia and Hebephilia are the same. The two paraphilias are distinctly different in relationship to age of the fantasy lover. Prepubescent children sexually arouse pedophiles while the hebephile is sexually aroused by youth at the age of puberty and adolescence. This distinction is significant, as a pedophile is generally not sexually aroused by a pubescent youth, and a prepubescent child does not sexually arouse a hebephile.

This distinction in age and sexual maturity plays an important part in identification of offender groups. The pedophile is apt to visit the playgrounds of elementary schools and the hebephile is apt to be found lurking at athletic fields of the junior high school. The two paraphiliacs do not mix their desired fantasy lover groups. Similarly, the two paraphiliacs have a tendency to be gender specific and do not mix the genders of their fantasies. Consequently, the behavior of a pedophile and a hebephile is based on the characteristics of the victim.

If an incident of inappropriate sexual behavior takes place with a stranger and a minor child, one can predict that the future behaviors of the offender will be directed at similar age and gender victims in locations where these children or youth are commonly found. The need for heightened levels of stimulation drives pedophiles and hebephiles to a point of obsessive-compulsive behavior. These paraphiliacs become obsessed with finding their fantasy lover and compulsively search for them.

Pedophiles and hebephiles interviewed in prison admit that their waking life is obsessed with fantasy urges and desires. Their sexuality is consumed by the paraphilias. Their total state of consciousness is overwhelmingly absorbed by thoughts of their fantasy lover.

It is difficult for people who are not afflicted with Pedophilia or Hebephilia to comprehend the concept of total obsession. In director Adrian Lyne's 1998 Trimark film production of Vladimir Nabokov's 1955 novel *Lolita*, actor Jeremy Irons brilliantly demonstrates the obsessive nature of Hebephilia. The totality of his conscious existence is overwhelmed by his obsession for Lolita.

As if addicted, these paraphiliacs obsess over their next opportunity to find their lover. If the afflicted person has experienced a sexual encounter with a child representative of his fantasy group, the obsession increases, pushing him to great extremes to meet his next lover.

This compulsive need drives him outside of his home to the locations where his potential fantasy lover may be located. It is this characteristic of the paraphilia that assists parents, teachers, law enforcement officers, and other childcare professionals to identify the pedophile and hebephile. However, if these adults are uninformed, inattentive, and/or complacent, the potential offender can go unnoticed and continue to search through his preferred fantasy groups.

The DSM-IV-TR notes:

> Individuals may limit their activities to their own children, stepchildren, or relatives or may victimize children outside their families. . . . Others, particularly those who frequently victimize children, develop complicated techniques for obtaining access to children, which may include winning the trust of a child's mother, marrying a woman with an attractive child, trading children with other individuals with Pedophilia, or in rare instances, taking in foster children from non-industrialized countries or abducting children from strangers. (p. 571)

While the DSM-IV-TR identifies some rather extreme mechanisms that afflicted persons may utilize, it neglects to identify the most obvious and potentially dangerous mechanism: Pedophiles and hebephiles make career, volunteer, and hobby decisions based on the potential presence of the relevant child fantasy group.

The best way to observe a large group of potential victims is to include oneself in a requisite or voluntary interest of the children. Because children are required to attend school, pedophiles and hebephiles find employment as teachers, teacher's aides, lunchroom and playground attendants, crossing guards, janitors, and bus drivers. School districts are careful in the hiring process of teachers, but the background searches of employment candidates for other positions is severely lacking. The pressing need to fill vacancies at critical, nonacademic positions often results in a lackadaisical interview and reference check process. The selection process is even worse at the volunteer level.

Pedophiles and hebephiles can gain access to children and youth by volunteering to serve in a variety of capacities in an elementary or junior high school. Overworked and complacent principals, teachers, and coaches are ecstatic when an adult volunteers to serve as a reading tutor, a library assistant, or an assistant soccer coach. The educator is happy for the assistance and the pedophile or hebephile has found his dream capacity.

Schools are not the only institutions that are targets for these paraphiliacs. Community agencies commonly scrutinize volunteers even less than schools do. And pedophiles know this. Large national organizations such as Boy Scouts and Girl Scouts, Big Brothers/Big Sisters, and the YMCA have rigid rules for volunteerism, with well-established screening processes born out of serious previous experiences. Still, unless a documented history of sexual misconduct with children turns up, pedophiles and hebephiles can easily slip through the process.

Smaller community organizations not affiliated with national organizations or the school districts are even more vulnerable. Paraphiliacs know which organizations are anxious for volunteer help. The local cubmaster in a small community, a volunteer himself, becomes desperate to find den masters as more boys want to participate in Cub Scouts and no parents accept volunteer roles. The college student in his early 20s who demonstrates his interest in helping out is welcomed with enthusiasm. Similarly, the parent who agrees to develop an age group baseball or soccer league or age group swim team is desperate for a sufficient number of coaches, timers, and other volunteers to meet the need of the number of children who want to participate. Older high school and college students are actively recruited to fill the void when parents refuse to participate. Flyers expressing the need for volunteer coaches are posted at the local community college. Pedophiles and hebephiles automatically know the age and gender of the participating children. The desperation of the group's chairperson to locate assistance is also obvious. The screening process will be nonexistent. The paraphiliac is welcomed and has instant access to his desired victim group.

The United States has recently been shocked by the indictment and conviction of Roman Catholic priests for cases of molesting children and youth. This has been misconstrued as an indictment of the Roman Catholic Church and the priesthood profession. The denomination and the honorable profession have been smeared by a minuscule number of offenders and the media. It is illogical to assume that pedophiles and hebephiles are attracted to the priesthood for access to children. Pedophiles and hebephiles who are compulsively looking to find their fantasy lovers are not willing to defer their gratification until they have completed many years of formal seminary education. They have immediate access to children through hundreds of alternative methods.

Some pedophiles and hebephiles are attracted to volunteer capacities within organized religion. Parents, encouraging their children's involvement in their community church, enthusiastically endorse their participation in choir, altar service, and youth groups. Ministers encourage volunteerism by their parishioners as service to the church. Consequently, pedophiles and hebephiles, as members of the congregation, volunteer in the nursery, as Sunday school teachers, and as youth group assistants to the youth pastor. Overburdened with demand for the service and confident of their intent to serve, the church welcomes these paraphiliac volunteers with open arms and praise.

The monumental disclosures by the Roman Catholic Church has produced repercussions throughout established religion. Congregations now scrutinize their professional and volunteer staffs, and the rates for liability insurance for acts of sexual misconduct by church personnel have reached new heights. The churches are also examining their service delivery systems to other populations.

Pastoral counseling is a service offered formally and informally in most churches, regardless of size or denomination. Larger churches have formal counseling services available to members of the congregation, who are often hesitant to seek counseling services from secular counselors, psychologists, and psychiatrists. The cost of private counseling is often prohibitive and the thought of airing their emotional problems produces anxiety in most individuals. Services without expense, the assurance of anonymity, and the trust in their church's pastor are appealing to those who are apprehensive to enter into a counseling relationship in the first place. The pastor/therapist in larger churches is commonly trained in pastoral counseling and, in many cases, these practitioners hold advanced degrees in counseling and psychotherapy. Ethics education is requisite to advanced degrees, training in pastoral counseling, and licensure. Incidents of ethics violations and malpractice occur with some frequency in the private sector and there is no reason to assume that similar violations do not take place in pastoral counseling. Sexual interaction with clients is a serious violation of ethics due to the vulnerability of the client and the transference common to therapy. Sexual misconduct in pastoral counseling is compounded by the trusting cleric–client relationship.

Smaller churches do not have the revenue to offer formal counseling services from a minister academically prepared in counseling and psychotherapy. Commonly, small congregations have insufficient revenue to hire their own minister and sometimes share the salary and benefits with another congregation. Ministers whose pulpit, administrative, and counseling skills are limited cannot command a large salary and therefore find employment in small churches. They may be required to provide pastoral services for which they have inadequate skill or training. Premarital, illness, grief, and family counseling services are required of them. Congregation members with limited resources also turn to the pastor for counseling on marital problems.

Whenever a therapist—secular or religious—provides counseling to a person who is seeking comfort and advice pertaining to marital or relationship problems, the potential for sexual misconduct increases. The therapist is viewed as a caring, empathetic person who actively listens with interest. Searching for answers to relationship problems, the client commonly develops feelings of affection for the caring therapist. The transference of love to the therapist is a problem frequently encountered in counseling relationships. It is ludicrous to believe that ministers are never involved in ethics violations involving sexual misconduct with a client.

Ministers are perceived not just as the worship leaders, but the epitome of moral standards. Many parishioners look to their minister to assist in solving their life problems; they trust them implicitly. They openly discuss marital and relationship problems with their ministers and ask their advice. Many blindly follow their minister's advice without question. Ministers in these roles find themselves held in regard, honor, and respect above the level of normal men, and some are influenced by this delusion of grandeur. Fundamental religious leaders Jimmy Swaggart and Jim Bakker are examples of ministers who were influenced by delusions of grandeur.

It also must be recognized that these clerical positions attract individuals with personality disorders who make career decisions that are made in relationship to fleecing the flock.

Part II

PERSONALITY DISORDERS

Chapter 8

Conduct Disorder, Antisocial Personality Disorder

CONDUCT DISORDER

Scenario

James, age 14, is sitting in the precinct station house handcuffed to the chair. He is waiting his mother's arrival from work before the detective can interrogate him. Protected as a juvenile by state statute, he cannot be questioned in the absence of a parent, guardian, or an attorney.

James is alleged to have forcefully and without consent fondled a female classmate in the hallway of the high school. James has been previously expelled for truancy, swearing at a teacher, smoking in the bathroom, and fighting. James is currently on probation for assaulting a rival gang member with a baseball bat. James' prior criminal charges include shoplifting, curfew violation, domestic violence on his mother, and possession of marijuana. James has been incarcerated in the community juvenile detention center on two prior occasions.

James is accurately diagnosed as a *Conduct Disordered* youth.

ANTISOCIAL PERSONALITY DISORDER

Scenario

Robert, age 40, is a successful business owner with an annual six-figure salary. However, his lifestyle exceeds his declared income. Robert juggles the expense account, writes off his family vehicles, files fraudulent tax returns, and blatantly violates a variety of government regulations to increase his profit.

Robert has had a string of affairs that he has successfully hidden from his wife. His frequent out of town business trips provide him with the opportunity for infidelity. He is completely egocentric and has no remorse for his behaviors. His conduct is driven by his egocentricity, his absence of conscience, and his personal need for pleasure and excitement. Only his personal interests are significant to him and he will behave in whatever fashion he desires, with no regard for the interest or safety of others.

Robert feels no guilt or regrets. He experiences anxiety only when the consequences for his behavior are frightening and close in proximity. He is a pathological liar and will concoct excuses and blame others to avoid detection and apprehension. The end justifies all the means necessary to accomplish his goals. Robert possesses an *Antisocial Personality Disorder*.

Personality Disorders Explained

Persons diagnosed with one or more of the sexual paraphilias may also be afflicted with a personality disorder that will exacerbate the paraphilia and significantly influence the behavioral manifestation of the paraphilia.

While the previous chapters of this book focused on discussions of sexual paraphilias and gender identity disorders, Chapters 8 and 9 will increase the scope of the discussion of sexual predators by examining personality disorders.

The DSM-IV-TR specifies, defines, and discusses ten specific personality disorders. "A personality disorder is an enduring pattern of inner experience and behavior that deviates markedly from the expectations of the individual's culture, is pervasive and inflexible, has an onset in adolescence or early adulthood, is stable over time, and leads to distress or impairment" (p. 685).

Personality disorders are difficult for nonclinically trained persons to understand. The characteristic behaviors of those having many of the disorders are disturbing and laypersons consider these persons "crazy," or mentally ill. In reality, persons diagnosed with personality disorders are not mentally ill in clinical terms. Rather, they are fully cognizant of their behaviors, which often are utilized to produce a desired result. In other words, the behaviors of the personality disordered individual are purposeful, while it is common that the behaviors of mentally ill persons are not purposeful.

The DSM-IV-TR establishes the following general criteria for a personality disorder:

A. An enduring pattern of inner experience, and behavior that deviates markedly from the expectations of the individual's culture. This pattern is manifested in two (or more) of the following areas:

   (1) Cognition (i.e., ways of perceiving and interpreting self, other people, and events)

   (2) Affectivity (i.e., the range, intensity, lability, and appropriateness of emotional response)

   (3) Interpersonal functioning

   (4) Impulse control

B. The enduring pattern is inflexible and pervasive across a broad range of personal and social situations.

C. The enduring pattern leads to clinically significant distress or impairment in social, occupational, or other important areas of functioning.

D. The pattern is stable and of long duration, and its onset can be traced back at least to adolescence or early adulthood.

E. The enduring pattern is no better accounted for as a manifestation or consequence of another mental disorder.

F. The enduring pattern is not due to the direct physiological effects of a substance (e.g., a drug of abuse, a medication) or a general medical condition (e.g., head trauma). (p. 689)

Each of these general criteria for a personality disorder will be examined and explained using examples.

A personality disorder is described as an enduring pattern of experience and behavior that falls outside of society's definition of appropriate. Individuals afflicted with a personality disorder may perceive themselves differently from the way others view them. They may also interpret events differently than others interpret them. These perceptions, interpretations, and ensuing behaviors are determined by the individual to be correct and appropriate. A personality disordered individual is considered egosyntonic, that is, consistent with the individual's ego. In other words, personality disordered persons find their perceptions and interpretations accurate and their behavior appropriate, because the behaviors are congruent to their ego. Their perceptions, interpretations, and behaviors are in harmony with their ego and, therefore, are accurate and appropriate. If these individuals believed that their perceptions, interpretations, and behaviors were not in harmony with their egos, they would change them. This congruence to their ego makes it possible for them to conduct themselves in a fashion that is contrary to everyone around them, while still believing they are correct. This is also the most difficult aspect for nonclinical persons to understand.

The perceptions, interpretations, and behaviors of the disordered person are obviously inappropriate to the nondisordered persons observing them; however, the disordered persons not only believe themselves to be appropriate, but also continue the behaviors in the face of adversity. It appears illogical to nondisordered persons but it is logical to the disordered person. Despite being caught in obvious deceit and presented with supporting evidence, disordered persons will not accept it. They will resort to statements alleging conspiracy or question the validity of the evidence rather than conceding that they are wrong, which would be incongruent to their ego.

Conduct Disorder Defined

Conduct Disorder is reserved for persons under the age of 18 who have demonstrated a history of similar repetitive behavior. Conduct Disorder is described in two subgroups: childhood onset and adolescent onset. These subgroups are obviously a designation of age at the time of onset.

The DSM-IV-TR describes the diagnostic criteria for Conduct Disorder as follows:

A repetitive and persistent pattern of behavior in which the basic rights of others or major age-appropriate societal norms or rules are violated, as manifested by the presence of three (or more) of the following criteria in the past 12 months, with at least one criterion in the past six months:

Aggression to people and animals

1. Often bullies, threatens or intimidates others

2. Often initiates physical fights

3. Has used a weapon that can cause serious physical harm to others (e.g., a bat, brick, broken bottle, knife, gun)

4. Has been physically cruel to people

5. Has been physically cruel to animals

6. Has stolen while confronting a victim (e.g., mugging, purse snatching, extortion, armed robbery)

7. Has forced someone into sexual activity

Destruction of property

8. Has deliberately engaged in fire setting with the intention of causing serious damage

9. Has deliberately destroyed other's property (other than by fire setting)

Deceitfulness or theft

10. Has broken into someone else's house, building or car

11. Often lies to obtain goods or favors or to avoid obligations (i.e., "cons" others)

12. Has stolen items of nontrivial value without confronting a victim (e.g., shoplifting, but without breaking and entering; forgery)

Serious violations of rules

13. Often stays out at night despite parental prohibitions, beginning before age 13 years

14. Has run away from home overnight at least twice while living in parental or parental surrogate home (or once without returning for a lengthy period)

15. Is often truant from school, beginning before age 13 years (p. 99)

The American Psychiatric Association indicates that these sets of behavior are significant to diagnoses of Conduct Disorder, childhood onset type and adolescent type. Remember, the person must be under 18 years of age to be diagnosed as such. However, if the behavioral issues pertaining to school attendance, incorrigibility, and runaway are removed from the diagnostic criteria for Conduct Disorder, the remaining criteria are certainly not limited to the domain of persons under the age of 18. Given this reduced set of criteria, many persons well into their 20s and 30s could be diagnosed as Conduct Disordered.

The prisons of the United States are overwhelmingly overcrowded and the age group of 18 to 25 is overrepresented in comparison to the remaining inmate population. In examination of this inmate population, two issues are readily apparent:

1. In order to be incarcerated in a prison for adults, the inmate must have violated the law after the age of legal determination of being considered an adult in the state criminal code or must have committed a sufficiently heinous crime as a juvenile to be waived to the adult jurisdiction for prosecution and subsequent sentencing. Further, these inmates have all committed felonies.

2. Despite their chronological age, which prohibits their diagnosis as a Conduct Disorder, their behaviors are exactly those described as the criteria for a diagnosis of Conduct Disorder.

Consequently, the efficacy of the age criterion for Conduct Disorder is in question. Perhaps the behavioral manifestations of Conduct Disorder continue into adulthood. The impulsive aggressiveness commonly associated with Conduct Disordered adolescents with little or no concern for the safety and well being of others influences behavior beyond the age of 18. Taking the inquiry a step further: Does adolescence, in many cases, continue into the 20s and 30s? Perhaps the difference between Conduct Disorder and Antisocial Personality Disorder is better differentiated by maturity, sophistication, and—perhaps—intelligence, in contrast to chronological age. Examining the diagnostic criteria for Antisocial Personality Disorder will shed additional light on this inquiry.

Antisocial Personality Disorder Defined

The specific diagnostic criteria for Antisocial Personality Disorder are as follows:

There is a pervasive pattern of disregard for and violation of the rights of others occurring since age 15 years, as indicated by three (or more) of the following:

1. Failure to conform to social norms with respect to lawful behaviors as indicated by repeatedly performing acts that are grounds for arrest

2. Deceitfulness, as indicated by repeated lying, use of aliases or conning others for personal profit or pleasure

3. Impulsivity or failure to plan ahead

4. Irritability and aggressiveness, as indicated by repeated physical fights or assaults

5. Reckless disregard for the safety of self or others

6. Consistent irresponsibility, as indicated by repeated failure to sustain consistent work behavior or honor financial responsibilities

7. Lack of remorse, as indicated by being indifferent to or rationalizing having hurt, mistreated, or stolen from another (p. 706)

These criteria are specific to persons who are at least 18 years of age and have demonstrated a history of the Conduct Disorder behaviors discussed in the previous section.

The seriousness of Conduct Disorder and the Antisocial Personality Disorder is demonstrated through a blend of the diagnostic criteria and examination of behavioral manifestations. The seriousness of the disorders is exacerbated by comorbidity with sexual paraphilias.

The diagnostic criteria for Conduct Disorder identifies aggressive behavior such as initiating physical fights, utilizing weapons, and forcing sexual activity as significant. The blending of these behaviors with a wanton disregard for social norms, a violation of laws, and a disregard for the safety and well being of others increases the seriousness of the conduct. The impulsivity and lack of remorse for injuring others indicate that these individuals do not consider the impact of their behavior on others and do not care. The egocentricity and conscience deficiency characteristics of these disorders permit the individuals to perform with little or no remorse behaviors that are injurious to others. This lack of concern and remorse is further demonstrated in their pathological lying to avoid responsibility and consequences for their actions.

These individuals are not mentally ill, but their blatant disregard for social norms makes others consider them unbalanced. A trite but common response from onlookers is, "How can anyone in their right mind even consider doing a behavior like that?" The daily news is filled ad nauseam with behavioral manifestations of persons afflicted with these personality disorders.

Consider the comorbidity of Antisocial Personality Disorder with the paraphilia of Sexual Sadism. The resulting behavioral manifestations include aggravated rape with an implement, torture, and lust homicide. Consider the further seriousness of the behaviors if the above disorders are also comorbid with Pedophilia. The victim becomes a child.

Antisocial Personality Disorder is chronic and lifelong. As it is not a mental illness, there is no successful rehabilitative intervention. The individual chooses to do the behavior because he wants to and he derives pleasure from it. If he did not derive pleasure from the behavior, he would not do it. The behavior is willful and malicious. The only reason Antisocial Personality Disordered persons will change their behavior is because they find the consequence for the behavior personally painful. They stop the behavior to eliminate the potential for the consequence. They do not stop the behavior because they are convinced of the immorality of the behavior or feel regret and remorse for their conduct against the victim. Their egocentricity convinces them that they are more intelligent than the persons who are investigating the crimes, and that they will not be apprehended. Consequently, they continue to perform the behaviors.

The Antisocial Personality Disordered person who openly, repeatedly, and with impunity violates the law is obvious. However, a greater number of individuals afflicted with Antisocial Personality Disorder commit their behaviors—both lawful and unlawful—in a much more covert manner. The higher the level of intelligence of persons with Antisocial Personality Disorder, the more covert is their behavior.

The husband who repeatedly has affairs with other women, lies to his wife, and demonstrates no feelings of remorse for either his wife or the casual sex partner may very well be diagnosed with the disorder. The politician who accepts bribes for votes, the corporate executive who doctors the books, and the used car salesman who turns back the odometer on a vehicle are all demonstrating some of the diagnostic criteria for Antisocial Personality Disorder. They are not committing heinous crimes, however, their disregard for social norms is obvious. Deceitfulness regarding the behavior further demonstrates the criteria for the diagnosis.

However, in the context of this book, it is the Conduct Disordered or Antisocial Personality Disordered persons who stalk and sexually assault unsuspecting victims that we must be watchful for. The person who commits sexual assault, rape, and lust homicide with no feelings of guilt or remorse is dangerous and will commit the crimes repeatedly until he is apprehended.

Chapter 9

Paranoid, Borderline, Histrionic, Narcissistic Personality Disorders

PARANOID PERSONALITY DISORDER

Scenario

Tired of being singled out for ridicule by her work associates, Lisa quits her job. They will no longer be able to use her as a scapegoat for their personal dissatisfactions with life. This will show them. They will have to find someone else to gossip about. Lisa packs up her personal items from her desk, accuses her best friend of being disloyal, and storms out of the office.

As she waits for the bus, she attempts to ignore the strangers staring at her. She gives the bus driver a five-dollar bill and he only returns a quarter. He has shortchanged her four dollars and she loudly accuses him. The driver attempts to assure her that she only gave him a dollar by showing her the currency in his hand. He has cleverly switched the bill. The crowd behind her begins to complain about her holding up the line and reluctantly she drops her argument. Once again, someone else has successfully cheated her.

She gives the bus driver an angry look as she exits the bus two blocks from her apartment. She is confident that the man that was seated behind her has been following her for several weeks attempting to find out where she lives. In response to the stalker, she has been changing her routine by varying her time of departure for work and rotating the bus stops.

Lisa quickly walks around the block, glancing at her apartment entrance from across the street. She looks up and down the street and when she is sure she does not see the stalker, she crosses the street, enters the building, and scurries up the three flights of stairs to her apartment. The transparent tape that she put on the door jamb is still intact. No one has entered her apartment while she was at work. Lisa opens the door, quickly enters, and triple bolts the door behind her. She has successfully made it home.

This is the lifestyle of a person with a *Paranoid Personality Disorder.*

Paranoid Personality Disorder Defined

The DSM-IV-TR defines Paranoid Personality Disorder as "a pattern of pervasive distrust and suspiciousness of others such that their motives are interpreted as malevolent" (p. 690). Persons afflicted with this disorder possess some or all of the following diagnostic criteria:

1. Suspects, without sufficient basis, that others are exploiting, harming, or deceiving him or her
2. Is preoccupied with unjustified doubts about the loyalty or trustworthiness of friends or associates
3. Is reluctant to confide in others because of unwarranted fear that the information will be used maliciously against him or her
4. Reads hidden demeaning or threatening meanings into benign remarks or events
5. Persistently bears grudges, i.e., is unforgiving of insults, injuries, or slights
6. Perceives attacks on his or her character or reputation that are not apparent to others and is quick to react angrily or to counterattack
7. Has recurrent suspicions, without justification, regarding fidelity of spouse or sexual partner (p. 694)

Paranoid Personality Disorder Explained

Before any further discussion of Paranoid Personality Disorder takes place, it is significant to distinguish it from the mental illness of Paranoid Schizophrenia. The delusional characteristics of persecution and jealousy are common to both Paranoid Personality Disorder and Paranoid Schizophrenia, however, the person afflicted with the latter commonly experiences hallucinations.

> The essential feature of the Paranoid Type of Schizophrenia is the presence of prominent delusions or auditory hallucinations in the context of a relative preservation of cognitive functioning and affect. . . . Delusions are typically persecutory or grandiose, or both, but delusions with other themes (e.g., jealousy, religiosity, or somatization) may occur. . . . Hallucinations are also typically related to the content of the delusional theme. Associated features include anxiety, anger, aloofness and argumentativeness. . . . The persecutory themes may predispose the individual to suicidal behavior, and the combination of persecutory and grandiose delusions with anger may predispose the individual to violence. (DSM-IV-TR, 2000, p. 313–314)

The presence of hallucinations is the primary criterion that differentiates the Paranoid Personality Disorder from the Paranoid Type of Schizophrenia. Individuals afflicted with Paranoid Schizophrenia experience voices that are persecutory in nature and may direct them to perform antisocial and sometimes violent behaviors.

While the person afflicted with a Paranoid Personality Disorder may not experience the hallucinations, the pervasive distrust and suspiciousness of others may lead to aggressive and violent behavior. The pervasive distrust characteristic to this disorder prevents the individual from forming close social and intimate relationships. Such persons have a tendency to avoid social situations that include a number of people, particularly where cliques are established within the group.

Persons suffering from this disorder imagine that others are talking about them, and an unintentional glance or gesture in their direction reinforces this paranoid perception. While they are interested in developing social and intimate relationships with others, the process is anxiety producing. They are more apt to identify with others who appear to be alone and seeking companionship. They will readily engage the lone individual in a social or work environment and may even test the waters by making a negative comment about the social clique they feel is whispering about them. If the remark is received without rebuttal, an ally has been found. The disordered person will be less apprehensive and may pursue topics of conversation that are slightly off mainstream thought and prejudicial in nature. As the conversation continues, interest in forming a bond increases.

Individuals afflicted with this disorder commonly bond together and form their own social groups. They may appear similar to a cult, minimally possessing superficially similar views. Not willing to discard their newly established social group, they develop group thought and group behavior. If an individual within the group protests the apparent ideology or suggested group behavior, the aggregate group views the individual suspiciously, and he may be excluded. In examination of domestic terrorist groups endemic to the United States, the aggregate sense of paranoia is present.

A strong charismatic leader who suggests that the federal government is attempting to take away individual gun ownership as a mechanism to reduce the citizenry's ability to overthrow a corrupt government finds an enthusiastic group of followers in the persons afflicted with Paranoid Personality Disorder. The need for belonging to a group that they perceive does not reject them develops a solidarity based on paranoia and conspiracy. Failure to follow the ideology and the set of requisite behaviors results in an individual's being the subject of the group's distrust. Consequently, maintaining the relationship with the group meets the individual needs and pathology of the disordered person. It is a safe harbor among persons of the same disorder.

The individual or group behavior appears appropriate until a new association (person) is introduced. The individual, as well as the group, immediately reassumes the position of mistrust. The aggregate distrust of the group is obvious. They demand that the individual demonstrate his loyalty to their ideologies. Generally, words alone are an insufficient demonstration and the new associate must behaviorally demonstrate his trustworthiness by an act of self-mutilation, or an overt act of violence against the group's perceived enemy.

Individuals who have developed personal relationships with others become distrustful when a new person is introduced into the relationship. The disordered person immediately reassumes his attitude of distrust to both parties. He views his initial acquaintance as disloyal, and in the situation of an intimate relationship, may accuse the partner of infidelity. The delusional quality increases in severity and the disordered person begins to conjure clandestine activities between the other parties. Jealousy erupts and violent behavior may ensue. Perceptions become more skewed by the jealousy, simple comments or gestures are greatly over-exaggerated, and hostile feelings occur.

If the disordered person has also developed a delusional belief regarding the depth of the relationship, the feelings of jealousy, distrust, and hostility are amplified. A casual sexual relationship may be perceived as much more intimate and meaningful to the Paranoid Personality Disordered person. Consequently, discontinuation of the intimacy will result in distrust, rejection, jealousy, and hostile feelings. Persons afflicted with this disorder, when striving to develop a meaningful relationship with a person they trust, misconstrue simple gestures of friendliness and courtesy. A casual conversation between two classmates during a class break, a thoughtful gesture of kindness in carrying another's groceries, or cordiality in the workplace can be misconstrued by the disordered person that there is more to the relationship than there really is.

The realization that there is less or nothing to the relationship will precipitate distrust, jealousy, and hostile feelings. The innocent first date that ends in date rape may have been fueled by the misperceptions of a Paranoid Personality Disordered person. The afflicted person who is searching for a meaningful relationship invariably stalks the person he believes is his intended lover.

BORDERLINE PERSONALITY DISORDER

Scenario

Brenda looks adoringly into Mike's eyes and thanks him for a wonderful evening. Brenda is sure that Mike has enjoyed it as much as she has and feels the same chemistry that she feels. Brenda asks Mike if he would like to come up for a drink. Mike agrees and shortly thereafter they complete their first date with passionate lovemaking.

Mike rises from the bed and informs Brenda that he must leave because he has an early call in the morning. Brenda, reluctant for Mike to leave, begs him to stay the night and go directly to work from her apartment in the morning. Flattered by her offer, he promises to call her in the morning after his meeting. Mike kisses Brenda on the forehead and wishes her a good night's sleep.

Following the morning's meeting, Mike returns to his office. His secretary gives him three phone messages from Brenda. Smiling to himself, he closes his office door and calls Brenda. Yes, he will see her tonight and will pick her up around eight. The evening's date ends the same as the previous evening, but Brenda protests his departure from her bed. Concerned with her irrational demand that he stay, Mike tells her that he will call her to-morrow to discuss their weekend plans.

Busy throughout the day, Mike is unable to return any of Brenda's numerous phone calls. Her persistence is disturbing and Mike begins to believe that Brenda has made more of this relationship than he has. He chooses not to return her calls and spends the evening watching basketball with some male friends. Following an enjoyable evening he returns to his apartment to find his answering machine overflowing with messages from Brenda. Her final message indicates that if he does not call her, he will be responsible for her death.

Mike calls Brenda, who is crying hysterically. She asks him to come to her apartment. Mike is caught in the dilemma. If he goes to her apartment, he will reinforce her delusion that he loves her. If he does not go, she might truly commit suicide. Brenda's pathological fear of rejection and abandonment is characteristic of the *Borderline Personality Disorder*.

Borderline Personality Disorder Defined

The DSM-IV-TR describes the Borderline Personality Disorder as "a pattern of instability of interpersonal relationships, self-image, and affects, and marked impulsivity that begins in early adulthood and is present in a variety of contexts" (p. 706). This disorder is characterized by serious reaction to interpersonal stress. The etiology of this reaction to interpersonal stress is a fear of abandonment or rejection. The self-worth of people with this disorder is contingent upon acceptance and relationships with others. When confronted with perceived rejection or abandonment, these individuals experience intense feelings of loss of self-worth and react with myriad behaviors in response to this perception. They may dramatically attempt self-change, demonstrate anger and violence—inwardly as well as outwardly projected—present extreme impulsivity, and appear in panic and despair.

Self-mutilation and suicide attempts are common demonstrations. The DSM-IV-TR outlines the following diagnostic criteria for the Borderline Personality Disorder:

A pervasive pattern of instability of interpersonal relationships, self-image, and affects, and marked impulsivity beginning by early adulthood and present in a variety of contexts, as indicated by five (or more) of the following:

1. Frantic efforts to avoid real or imagined abandonment

2. A pattern of unstable and intense interpersonal relationships characterized by alternating between extremes of idealization and devaluation

3. Identity disturbance: markedly and persistently unstable self-image or sense of self

4. Impulsivity in at least two areas that are potentially self-damaging (e.g., spending, sex, substance abuse, reckless driving, binge eating)

5. Recurrent suicidal behavior, gestures, or threats, or self-mutilating behavior

6. Chronic feelings of emptiness

7. Inappropriate, intense anger or difficulty controlling anger (e.g., frequent displays of temper, constant anger, recurrent physical fights)

8. Transient, stress-related paranoid ideation or severe dissociative symptoms (p. 710)

It is significant that the disorder is pervasive and invades all aspects of the individual's life. While not lifelong, it is chronic for periods of up to 10 years in duration.

Borderline Personality Disorder Explained

The behavioral manifestations of this disorder may include serious displays of temper and physical violence. It may be inwardly directed through self-mutilation and suicide attempts or it may be outwardly directed in violent acts against others. Considering the etiology of fear of rejection and abandonment, outwardly directed anger may result in violent acts against persons who reject them or attempt to escape the relationship.

The DSM-IV-TR reports that the disorder is diagnosed predominantly in females, lessening the threat of sexual assault. However, other acts of violence may prevail. Young women are more apt to self-mutilate, attempt suicide, binge eat, and engage in sexual promiscuity as a behavioral manifestation of the disorder. While the possibility of sexual assault may be reduced, persons attempting to dissolve an intimate relationship with a Borderline Personality Disordered person may be victims of violent acts. This is encountered in both opposite and same gender relationships. The party who chooses to leave the relationship may experience a serious assault from the partner who is afflicted with the disorder. Sexual assault at this time is nonconsensual and would legally be considered rape, regardless of marital status.

HISTRIONIC PERSONALITY DISORDER

Scenario

It is 10:50 A.M. and the service starts in ten minutes. The church is nearly filled to capacity and the congregation is quietly greeting each other. Just before the choir's procession, a family enters the building and walks down the center aisle to the front pew of the church. The father is dressed in a white shirt, tie, and dark pin-striped suit. The children follow in clean, appropriate clothing. The mother follows her family down the center aisle. The late arrival and march to the front pew has already drawn the attention of the entire congregation.

The mother is dressed in a black cocktail dress, cut low and showing her cleavage. Cut above the knee and with a slit up the side, her attractive thighs are exposed with every step. The heads of the men in congregation turn and admire the woman's figure and dress. The women of the congregation elbow their husbands and whisper their contempt for the woman's choice of attire for the church service.

The congregation has witnessed the seductive, attention seeking behavior of a *Histrionic Personality Disordered* woman.

Histrionic Personality Disorder Defined

The DSM-IV-TR describes "the essential feature of Histrionic Personality Disorder as pervasive and excessive emotionality and attention-seeking behavior. This pattern begins in early adulthood and is present in a variety of contexts" (p. 711). Histrionic Personality Disorder is diagnosed more frequently in women than men.

The salient and most obvious characteristic of this disorder is the need to be the center of attention. This need for attention is pervasive and invades all aspects of the individual's life. It is commonly chronic and life-long. The individual afflicted with this disorder utilizes a set of behaviors that are seductive, theatrical, and intended to draw attention to them.

The DSM-IV-TR identifies the following diagnostic criteria for the Histrionic Personality Disorder:

A pervasive pattern of excessive emotionality and attention seeking, beginning by early adulthood and present in a variety of contexts, as indicated by five (or more) of the following:

1. Is uncomfortable in situations in which he or she is not the center of attention
2. Interaction with others is often characterized by inappropriate sexually seductive or provocative behavior
3. Displays rapidly shifting and shallow expression of emotions
4. Consistently uses physical appearance to draw attention to self
5. Has a style of speech that is excessively impressionistic and lacking in detail
6. Shows self-dramatization, theatricality, and exaggerated expression of emotion
7. Is suggestible, i.e., easily influenced by others or circumstances
8. Considers relationships more intimate than they actually are (p. 714)

Histrionic Personality Disorder Explained

While the DSM-IV-TR indicates that men are also afflicted with this disorder, it is more commonly found in women. Men afflicted with this disorder may manifest the disorder in theatrical demonstrations of machismo, but in reality, they are merely demonstrations of sexuality. They dress in tight-fitting clothing, have expensive haircuts, and may even seek employment as male exotic dancers. This façade to attract women or gay men often results in confrontations with aggressive heterosexual alpha males who find these displays of sexuality effeminate and offensive. The aggressive male will confront the histrionic male with threats of violence that frighten the afflicted individual. Demands for demonstration of "toughness" are common but the histrionic male is incapable of withstanding the challenge. Consequently, the histrionic male avoids bars and workout gymnasiums frequented by aggressive alpha males. He instead frequents lounges of the "beautiful" people and "workout salons" where his demonstrations of sexuality are acknowledged and the challenge of aggressive males is absent.

A woman afflicted with this disorder carefully determines the locations where she can demonstrate her superiority in sexuality. She does not frequent locations or attend functions where she is in competition for center stage. A histrionic woman carefully selects her domain. She frequents bars where she is not in competition with other women, and where her presence attracts the attention of others. She enters the room with theatrics, demonstrating a provocative and seductive attitude. She dresses in seductive clothing just within the margin of acceptability for the occasion. If the prescribed attire is casual, she will wear short shorts and a tank top, clothing that accentuates and flatters her most attractive physical attributes. For black tie events, she will wear an article of clothing that accentuates her most seductive physical characteristic in order to draw the attention of men at the event. She may wear a low-cut dress that flatters her breasts, a dress with a slit up the side to call attention to her legs, or a form-fitting dress to accentuate her figure. Her make-up and hairstyle will highlight the attractive aspects of her facial features. It is her intent to be observed and acknowledged.

It is commonly held that women dress for the admiration of other women; however, a histrionic woman dresses for the admiration of men. Her physical appearance draws the attention of men and, subsequently, the criticism of other women. She demonstrates a dominant territoriality over the other women at the same event. It is her intent to demonstrate superiority in attractiveness and sexuality, and her self-worth is contingent upon the acknowledgement of this dominance.

Males are expected to acknowledge her presence and in the absence of this acknowledgement, a histrionic woman will increase the intensity of her theatrics. She will purposefully approach a group of men and engage them in conversation in a seductive tone of voice, demanding their attention. The late actor Marilyn Monroe was the epitome of a histrionic woman using voice tone and quality to demonstrate provocative sensuality. Her singing of "Happy Birthday" to President John F. Kennedy is a perfect example of how voice can be used as a provocative gesture.

Histrionic women who have drawn the attention of unattached males at an event also present themselves to males who attend with other women. Histrionic women are not satisfied just by the recognition from unattached males; they demand attention from all males so they can demonstrate their dominance over all the other women in attendance. These behaviors also draw the negative attention of other women. Two histrionic women at the same event equals a catastrophe waiting to happen, a potential battle of domination.

The pathology of the disorder increases in severity when a histrionic woman cannot dominate and be the center of attention. When she has exhausted her repertoire of theatrical behaviors, she may resort to creating a scene. She may manufacture a sudden illness requiring medical attention, an allegation of sexual misconduct on the part of another, or perhaps a threat of suicide. Actor Glenn Close, in the film *Fatal Attraction,* accurately portrays many of the behavioral manifestations of a woman afflicted with Histrionic Personality Disorder.

It is critical to examine the relationship between the Histrionic Personality Disorder and the potential for assault, rape, and lust homicide. The seductive behaviors of a person afflicted with Histrionic Personality Disorder may lead another to believe that the flirtation presented by the histrionic person is more sincere than it actually is, resulting in an aggressive date rape encounter. Histrionic men and women may also invite assault from the partners of those persons who are attracted to their flirtatious advances.

NARCISSISTIC PERSONALITY DISORDER

Scenario

The black luxury sedan pulls up to the valet parking and the 50-ish male driver waits for the attendant to open his door. He instructs the attendant to park the car in a spot where there is no possibility of another driver inadvertently opening a car door into the side of his car. Should that happen, he would personally see that the attendant is fired.

His date is strikingly beautiful and at least 15 years younger than him. He offers her his arm and they enter the elaborate hotel lobby. He requests that they be escorted to the hotel's five-star restaurant. The couple struts across the lobby and waits while the concierge announces his arrival to the maître d'. They are escorted to his table of choice and he informs the waiter that he will have "his usual" and to bring his date a glass of champagne.

Waiters, bus boys, and the bartender hustle around to avoid his sharp tongue. He returns his steak, requesting another because the first is over-cooked. At the end of the dinner, he calls over the maître d' to inform him that dinner was not up to their standards and that he expects rectification in his bill. The bar tab is subtracted from the evening's bill. As they depart, he does not offer a tip to the valet attendant.

He takes his date to her apartment and informs her that he is coming up for a drink. Unwilling to provide consensual sex, the man forces her to have intercourse as payment for the night's entertainment. This young woman has just experienced the characteristics of a *Narcissistic Personality Disorder.*

Narcissistic Personality Disorder Defined

The DSM-IV-TR describes the Narcissistic Personality Disorder as:

A pervasive pattern of grandiosity (in fantasy or behavior), need for admiration, and lack of empathy, beginning by early adulthood and present in a variety of contexts, as indicated by five (or more) of the following:

1. Has a grandiose sense of self-importance (e.g., exaggerates achievements and talents, expects to be recognized as superior without commensurate achievements)

2. Is preoccupied with fantasies of unlimited success, power, brilliance, beauty, or ideal love

3. Believes that he or she is "special" and unique and can only be understood by, or should associate with, other special or high-status people (or institutions)

4. Requires excessive admiration

5. Has a sense of entitlement, i.e., unreasonable expectations of especially favorable treatment or automatic compliance with his or her expectations

6. Is interpersonally exploitative, i.e., takes advantage of others to achieve his or her own ends

7. Lacks empathy: is unwilling to recognize or identify with the feelings and needs of others

8. Is often envious of others or believes that others are envious of him or her

9. Shows arrogant, haughty behaviors or attitudes (p. 717)

Narcissistic Personality Disorder Explained

Narcissistic Personality Disorder is more commonly diagnosed in men than in women. As the reader will notice, the Narcissistic Personality Disorder has a number of diagnostic criteria that are common to other personality disorders. When an individual demonstrates the diagnostic criteria of the Narcissistic Personality Disorder as well as the criteria for another disorder, both should be acknowledged.

The individual afflicted with this disorder views himself or herself as superior to others, possessing qualities that make him or her special and deserving to be admired by others. These qualities are exaggerations of the reality of the particular attribute; however, the disordered individual perceives them as accurate. When faced with the reality that they are not superior to others, they are seriously impacted. It is incongruent to their ego that they are not the "best" and superior to others. They cannot accept criticism and defeat. When faced with criticism and defeat, they will rely on defense mechanisms to counteract the sense of loss of self-worth.

These individuals will place the blame for failure on others with little or no concern for the well being of the person they have blamed. They excuse the possibility of their deficiency by placing it on another. They do not have empathy for the other person nor do they experience remorse for their action. They may also use anger and aggression to counterattack the criticism or defeat. If the confrontation is successful, the perception of superiority is maintained, in fact, probably reinforced. If they have been successful using a particular mechanism in previous situations of criticism or defeat, they will rely on it again. The husband who is caught in the act of infidelity may react angrily and aggressively toward his spouse to reduce his culpability. Threats or acts of violence that successfully curb the criticism are reinforced and the individual will employ them again in future confrontations. Not only does this behavior stop the criticism, but it also reinforces the person's perception of superiority.

When it is completely impossible to escape the criticism or defeat, those with this disorder may retreat into social isolation. The act of isolating themselves from the criticism or defeat protects their self-perception of superiority. Rather than engaging, they choose to isolate themselves from the criticizing individual. The narcissistic individual believes that the isolation makes the other person suffer because they have lost their companionship.

Individuals afflicted with Narcissistic Personality Disorder are usually easy to identify. Their sense of self-importance is demonstrated through their boasting and bragging mannerisms. They elevate themselves by bragging and diminish the presence of others through degrading comments. Their self-imposed sense of entitlement dictates that they be acknowledged upon entering a room, and not only praised for their abilities, but also given special privileges for them, privileges others are not worthy of receiving. They expect to be admired.

Men afflicted with Narcissistic Personality Disorders expect to be admired by women and coveted by other men. Expectations of admiration may include physical affection and sexual activity. Rejections of amorous advances are viewed as unacceptable and incongruent with the individual's ego. Rejection may result in anger, degrading insults, and nonconsensual sexual contact. In serious situations, the victim may be raped. The disordered person believes that he is entitled to the sexual contact and, when not consensually provided, may force it.

The most serious dual diagnosis of the personality disorders discussed in this chapter is the combination of the Antisocial Personality Disorder and the Narcissistic Personality Disorder. The blending of the grandiose sense of entitlement of the Narcissistic Personality Disorder with the failure to conform to social norms and reckless disregard for others of the Antisocial Personality Disorder may predispose such a person to sexual assault.

Part III

ATTACKS RELATED TO PARAPHILIAS AND PERSONALITY DISORDERS

Chapter 10

Stalking Patterns

Stalkers do not neatly fit into an established taxonomy. The behavior of stalking is unique to the individual's intent and/or personality and emotional disturbance. Due to the unique nature of the individual's circumstances, empirical study of the taxonomy system cannot be conducted unless individuals who do not neatly fit into any category are categorized arbitrarily. The construction of taxonomy ultimately results in the naming of the category, which often does not accurately describe the person who is stalking. Further, the titles utilized to name the category are not universally defined. "Celebrity" stalkers was a name ascribed to individuals who stalked celebrities such as movie stars, political officials, and others with face or name recognition. But "celebrity" stalker describes the victim rather than the person doing the stalking. It tells us little about the stalker. Rather than utilize an established taxonomy or construct a new one, this chapter focuses on understanding the intent, personality, and emotional status, and the overall nature of individuals who stalk.

Webster's Unabridged Dictionary (2001) defines stalk as "to pursue or approach prey, quarry, etc., stealthily" (p. 1855).

This definition merely describes the characteristics of an activity and the intent of conducting the activity without being detected.

The word "stalk" used to describe the behavior of one person toward another is generally considered an illegal activity, however, to be considered illegal, stalking must fit certain statutory requirements. A law enforcement officer in pursuit of a person for whom a search warrant has been authorized will attempt to locate the offender stealthily, without being detected. Such stalking behavior is considered "good practice" and reduces the possibility of a confrontation. The offender does not have time to prepare to elude or prevent his apprehension.

The behavior of stalking determined to be illegal is deviant, and it falls outside of socially acceptable or normative behavior. Most states clearly delineate in their criminal codes those stalking behaviors that are considered deviant, and they have established punitive measures to dissuade persons from performing the behavior. Clear delineation of the behavior protects the victim, as well as an innocent person who performs a similar behavior. A male college student who waits for a female student outside of her dormitory in hopes of asking her out for a date is engaged in an innocent activity. In contrast, if the female student has already rebuked the male college student for harassing her, he has fulfilled the statutory definition of stalking. Of the states that have enacted antistalking legislation, the definition and penalty for the behavior can differ.

Each state offers differing levels of protection from stalking behaviors. Many states have stalking statutes that are vague and do not protect victims. It is suggested that readers examine their state's statutes to determine the degree of protection and, if necessary, to lobby for stronger statutes and enforcement efforts. Three state statutes are examined below.

California Penal Code—Section 646.9

A knowing and willful course of conduct directed at a specific person that seriously alarms, annoys, torments, or terrorizes the person, and that serves no legitimate purpose.

Indiana Criminal Code—IC 35-45-2, Acts 1976, P.L. 148 Section 5

"Stalk" means a knowing or an intentional course of conduct involving repeated (3) or continuing harassment of another person that would cause a reasonable person to feel terrorized, intimidated or threatened and that actually causes the victim to feel terrorized, frightened, intimidated or threatened.

"Harassment" means conduct directed toward a victim that includes, but is not limited to, repeated or impermissible contact that would cause a reasonable person to suffer emotional distress.

"Impermissible Contact" includes but is not limited to intentionally pursuing or following the victim.

Penalties:

A. A person who stalks another person—Class D Felony—1 and ½ years' imprisonment.

B. A person stalks another person and makes an explicit or implicit threat with the intent to place the victim in reasonable fear of

1. Sexual assault

2. Serious bodily injury

3. Death

Class C Felony—4 years imprisonment

Florida Statute 784.048

(1) As used in this section, the term

a. "Harass" means to engage in a course of conduct directed at a specific person that causes substantial emotional distress in such person and serves no legitimate purpose.

b. "Course of Conduct" means a pattern of conduct composed of a series of acts over a period, however short, evidencing a continuity of purpose. Constitutionally protected activities are not included within the meaning of "course of conduct." Such constitutionally protected activity includes picketing or organized protests.

c. "Credible threat" means a threat made with the intent to cause the person who is the target of the threat to reasonably fear for his or her safety. The threat must be against the life of, or a threat to cause bodily injury to, a person.

(2) Any person who willfully, maliciously and repeatedly follows or harasses another person commits the offense of stalking, a misdemeanor, punishable as provided in s.775.082 or s.777.083.

Any person who willfully, maliciously, and repeatedly follows or harasses another person, and makes a credible threat with the intent to place that person in reasonable fear of death or bodily injury, commits the offense of aggravated stalking, a felony of the third degree, punishable as provided in s.775.082, s.775.083, or s.775.084.

Any person who, after an injunction for protection against repeat violence pursuant to s.784.046, or an injunction for protection against domestic violence pursuant to s.741.30, or after any other court-imposed prohibition of conduct toward the subject person or that person's property, knowingly, willfully, maliciously and repeatedly follows or harasses another person commits the offense of aggravated stalking, a felony of the third degree, punishable as provided in s.775.082, s.775.083, or s.775.084.

> 1. Any person who willfully, maliciously, and repeatedly follows or harasses a minor under 16 years of age commits the offense of aggravated stalking, a felony of the third degree, punishable as provided in s.775.082, s.775.083, or s.775.084.
>
> 2. Any law enforcement officer may arrest, without warrant, any person he or she has probable cause to believe has violated the provisions of this section.

The statutes of the three states differ in content, specificity, and extent of punishment. The stalking statutes define the states' legislative concern regarding the behavior. The California statute was one of the first drafted in the United States. The impetus for the legislative action was precipitated by acts of persons stalking Hollywood celebrities. In examining the statute, the significant legal elements can be identified. The statute specifies that the person engage in the behavior "willfully and knowingly," in contrast to doing it through ignorance or incompetence. Thus, the statute requires that there is purpose to the behavior and that it constitutes malicious intent.

The California statute also stipulates that the behavior not be a general pattern of behavior but directed at a specific person. An individual who follows numerous people who possess certain similarities may have illicit intent. However, as his/her behavior is not exclusive to a single individual, it is not considered stalking. This is not to say that the public should not be alarmed, but rather the inappropriate behavior should be reported to local law enforcement. The act of following a variety of individuals may be a demonstration of a person who has identified a particular victim group but has not identified a specific individual.

Generalized stalking is a serious behavior that must be brought to the attention of law enforcement officials, as it is the logical precursor to the stalking of an individual. In order to prosecute under the California statute, it is necessary for the stalking to be exclusive to one victim. Generalized stalking can be prosecuted under other definitions of criminal activity.

The California statute also specifies that the course of conduct "alarms, annoys, torments or terrorizes." This legal aspect is particularly significant because it indicates that it is the victim's perception that is critical, not the perception of the person engaged in the conduct, or that of law enforcement officers and prosecuting attorneys. If the individual who is the subject of the course of conduct "feels" alarmed, annoyed, tormented, or terrorized by the behavior, the legal element has been met. It is not necessary for others to substantiate the victim's perceptions and feelings. This element effectively removes discretion from the hands of law enforcement, prosecution, and defense counsel for the defendant. The victim's feelings and perceptions are considered valid until there is a legal finding otherwise. The victim's feelings and perception of threat are required to be acknowledged and not brushed aside as insignificant by responding officers.

The final legal element of the California statute protects persons who are engaged in a course of conduct that is legitimate. A process server attempting to deliver a summons to appear in court certainly fulfills the other legal elements of the statute, but the course of conduct has a legitimate purpose. Conversely, someone who engages in other legitimate activities that annoy or harass another might fit the legal element of the statute. The salesperson who makes repeated contacts with an individual who has rebuked him for his behavior may fit the legal definition for stalking.

The Indiana statute takes the course of conduct several steps further in its definition of stalking. This statute specifically identifies the number of occasions a person performs the course of conduct to qualify them for prosecution. The California statute indicates a "course of conduct" without any delineation of the number of illegitimate episodes that are required to meet the statute's requirements; this consequently becomes an issue of debate for prosecution and defense. Similarly, the Florida statute indicates "a pattern of conduct composed of a series of acts over time, however short, evidencing a continuity of purpose." The issues of "pattern," "series," and "over time" are subject to legal debate because they are not specified.

Indiana's establishment of a specific number of episodes requires documentation and clearly indicates that if there have been three reported and documented episodes of the conduct, then the victim has redress available in court. Further, the documentation of three episodes specifically meets a statutorily established criterion and prosecution of the perpetrator may commence.

Indiana's statute also utilizes the "reasonable man" theory as a standard for determining if the behavior in question warrants feelings of terror, fear, intimidation, or threat on the victim's part. A police officer's perception of conduct that precipitates fear and threat is likely much different from that of the senior citizen who lives alone. Consequently, the determination of feelings of terror, fear, intimidation, or threat is removed from the hands of law enforcement, prosecution, and defense and given to either a presiding judge or a jury of "reasonable" people. This assures that the victim's feelings are addressed from their perspective and it also protects the defendant from "unreasonable" allegations.

Finally, the Indiana statute specifically addresses the concept of "pattern of behavior" and "course of conduct" by utilizing and defining "impermissible contact." The statute specifically indicates that "impermissible" contact includes, but is not limited to, intentionally pursuing or following the victim. The statute specifies that intentional pursuing and following is impermissible contact; it also states that other behaviors may also be considered impermissible contact. Examples of these other impermissible contacts may include repeated phone calls and nonconsensual observing, such as parking one's vehicle across the street from the victim's house and watching the house.

The Florida statute is not as explicit as the Indiana and California statutes, and, consequently, it is often subject to legal challenges. As indicated previously, the Florida statute does not define "pattern," "series," or "over time" and therefore these legal elements may be subject to arbitrary and capricious definition. Minimally, they will be defined differently in every jurisdiction.

The Florida statute, however, does specify that constitutionally protected activities are not included in the "course of conduct." This presents an interesting inquiry and potential dilemma. The Bill of Rights provides for assurances that groups have the right to gather and conduct meetings. Obviously included in these constitutionally protected activities are church services, school athletic events, public auctions, and so on. Eliminating these gatherings from the course of conduct suggests that one may pursue or follow another as long as the conduct occurs at constitutionally protected activities. It is therefore illegal to follow or stalk someone in public except at constitutionally protected activities. This legal element is particularly significant in situations in which a restraining or no-contact order has been issued to someone found guilty of the stalking offense. This element suggests that the restraining or no-contact order is moot at constitutionally protected activities.

The Florida statute requires that a "credible threat" must exist, which is defined as "a threat made with intent to cause the person who is the target of the threat to reasonably fear for his or her safety." Therefore, a course of conduct that may include numerous episodes of nonconsensual watching in which there is no explicit credible threat does not fit the definition of stalking, regardless of the victim's feeling of implicit threat.

This analysis of stalking statutes from three states demonstrates that great disparity exists regarding the protection afforded victims. Some statutes clearly demonstrate victim advocacy, while some statutes are so poorly worded that law enforcement officers and prosecutors are handicapped in their ability to protect the victims of stalking episodes.

MOTIVATION FOR STALKING CONDUCT

The motivation to stalk another person is unique to the individual who is performing the conduct. Attempting to categorize persons who stalk others minimizes the significance of the individual's unique motivation, whether it is anger, frustration, sexual paraphilia, or delusions. Utilizing the Indiana stalking definition, one acknowledges that the conduct of stalking is exclusive to an individual victim, has occurred on at least three occasions, and is minimally threatening to the victim. Therefore, the conduct is willful and driven by a motivation. Failure to acknowledge and examine the motivation for the behavior may have serious implications.

Stalking meets the intrinsic needs of the stalker. The behavior would not be performed unless the person wanted to do it. In cases of illegitimate stalking, the person chooses to do the behavior. He or she stalks someone because doing so meets his or her personal needs. If there were no personal need to stalk, they would not choose the behavior. Thus, the inquiries are simple ones: Why are they doing the behavior? Why are they stalking this particular person? The answers to these two questions reflect the motivation of the stalker, and, therefore, the degree of severity and dangerousness of the behavior.

As indicated earlier in this chapter, there is no attempt to categorize or summarize stalking behavior. Rather, our goal is to examine and evaluate a variety of motivations and the behavioral manifestations of these motivations.

One of the most common motivations for stalking is an interest in changing the behavior of the victim. The victim demonstrates a behavior that the stalker disapproves of and is determined to change. There are hundreds of examples of this motivation and the specific behaviors employed by the stalker. A few will be discussed to enhance the knowledge and reduce the naiveté of the reader.

Both men and women can be stalkers. While stalking is commonly considered a male-exclusive activity, women also engage in it. The DSM-IV-TR indicates that with the exception of Sexual Masochism, the sexual paraphilias are generally considered male exclusive. However, stalking is not a course of conduct that is limited to persons afflicted with a sexual paraphilia. More commonly, persons who do not have a sexual paraphilia commit stalking. Stalking, in these cases, is a course of conduct used to change the behavior of the victim.

Men and women interested in finding social companions gather at locations where they might meet people of similar interest, age, and gender preference. College-age men and women attend classes not only to increase their education but also to meet people. The workplace, similar to the college setting, provides the opportunity for persons to socialize. Men and women interested in meeting new people frequent bars, health clubs, and athletic events. These settings provide the opportunity for the development of social acquaintances.

One interesting aspect of these initial encounters is that the parties rarely have the same level of understanding of the receptiveness of the other party. One person may believe the encounter was more significant than did the other party. One person believes there is more to the relationship. The other finds it to be only a causal acquaintance. This difference in level of perception can lead to a misunderstanding.

The person who perceives the relationship as meaningful attempts to advance it, and the other person, perceiving the relationship as causal, is not interested in advancing it. Advances may be rebuked. If there is a mutual perception that the relationship is worth exploring, the two persons will consensually advance it. The two may begin to date and the level of intimacy in the relationship may consensually increase.

Conflict arises when the perception of the significance of the relationship begins to differ. One party may begin to refuse further advancement of the relationship, while the other continues to pursue it, intolerant of a hiatus, or worse, a step backwards. The person who is interested in maintaining or advancing the relationship disapproves of the other party's reluctance and change in previous receptivity and behavior. The first person will attempt to change the second person's behavior to his or her interest. The person may attempt numerous mechanisms, some of which might involve intimidation to produce the desired result.

Despite being rebuked, the person might engage in stalking conduct—sending gifts, making repeated phone calls, driving by the other person's residence or workplace, and "showing up" at locations where an encounter is inevitable. More severe behaviors include following the other person, wiretapping phone lines, and Voyeurism. They might sneak around the person's residence peering into windows and park their vehicle across the street from their home or workplace. Obsessed persons will steal the victim's mail and go through their garbage to determine if they are dating someone else.

The situation is exacerbated if the uninterested party begins to date someone else. The rejected party may begin to stalk the new suitor, perhaps successfully curtailing the suitor's interest in the victim. The motivation for this course of stalking conduct is obvious and straightforward. It is intended to intimidate the victims and force them to change their behavior—specifically, return the relationship back to the prior status. It is a mechanism with intent to control and possess. If the stalking behavior successfully modifies the victim's position, the behavior is reinforced and it will be utilized again and as frequently as necessary.

The situation worsens because the stalker knows he/she has been successful in changing the behavior of the victim by using fear and intimidation. If the victim resurrects the courage to rebuke the stalker and ignore the stalking behavior, the stalker may increase the intensity of the fear-producing situation. The stalker may perform behaviors that suggest his/her ability to become violent. The stalker may make serious threats of bodily harm to the victim and to others close to the victim. It can be as subtle as meeting the victim's parent, child, best friend, or employer, or as overtly violent as smashing the windows of the victim's vehicle or killing her pet. Assaults on the victim are also common, particularly in cases of domestic violence. The majority of the women murdered in the United States each year die at the hands of a rejected suitor, lover, or husband, estranged or not.

The behaviors described in this discussion are extremely common and, in the absence of stalking statutes, they are successful in intimidating the victim to change his or her behavior. Stalking behaviors are also utilized to produce changes in the behavior of employers, teachers, and parents. Once the stalker successfully instills fear and intimidation into the victim, he or she will continue to use it for control. The elderly parent who is physically intimidated by his grown child relinquishes control of his person and property. The teacher intimidated by the teenager following her home from school relinquishes control of the classroom.

Numerous Hollywood productions have demonstrated stalking behaviors used to intimidate and produce change on the part of the victim. In *Fatal Attraction*, Glenn Close's character demonstrates obsessive, threatening, and violent behavior in stalking Michael Douglas' character. Close brilliantly portrays her character's delusional belief that the brief relationship she has with a married man is as significant to him as it is to her. When Michael Douglas' character rebukes her repeated attempts to advance the relationship, she increases the threat by stalking his wife and daughter and killing the family pet. This woman's motivation is obvious and clear-cut: She wants him to change his behavior and resume their relationship at the level she desires.

The remake of the movie *Cape Fear*, starring Robert DeNiro and Nick Nolte, is an excellent example of the use of revenge and retaliation as a motivation for stalking behavior. DeNiro's character stalks Nolte's character to produce fear in him. He stalks his wife, daughter, and girlfriend in demonstration of his anger at his former lawyer's failure to provide adequate counsel for him, which resulted in his imprisonment. The motivation is obvious and frank. He is angry and wants the lawyer to be frightened of him.

STALKING AND MENTAL ILLNESS

Stalking behavior may also be a behavioral manifestation of a mental illness. As discussed earlier, delusions that are symptomatic of some mental illnesses may precipitate stalking behaviors. John Hinckley, who attempted to assassinate President Ronald Reagan, was found to be mentally ill and incompetent to stand trial. It was also determined that Hinckley was not stalking President Reagan. Rather, his motivation for the attempted assassination was to impress actor Jodie Foster. Hinckley was delusional in his belief that Jodie Foster would actually love him and that she only needed to be convinced of the seriousness of his belief. Hinckley had attempted to contact Foster on numerous occasions but she rebuked his advances. The interesting inquiry is: Did Hinckley believe that by shooting the President, Jodie Foster would take notice of him, or was the shooting a statement of threat to Jodie Foster? Certainly if Hinckley could get close enough to Reagan to shoot him he could move close enough to Jodie Foster to shoot her. Did Hinckley believe that this implied threat was sufficient to make her change her opinion of him and her behavior?

Persons suffering from Paranoid Schizophrenia may have delusions that certain people are engaged in activities to hurt them, and it becomes necessary for them to stalk and preemptively strike for their own protection. Similarly, afflicted individuals may have delusions of conspiracies that cause them to engage in stalking behaviors. Some of these stalking behaviors by mentally ill persons are precipitated by auditory hallucinations. The "voices" associated with auditory hallucinations may be directing the individual to follow and perhaps even harm other people. Other stalking behaviors are precipitated by an individual's personality disorder.

THE HISTRIONIC PERSONALITY

As we have seen, persons with Histrionic Personality Disorder need to be at the center of attention, and when they find that they are not, they will use some dramatic flair to accomplish their goal. When rejected as the center of attention, particularly when in competition for a romantic relationship, they will pursue the individual, often with inappropriate, sexually provocative, and seductive behavior. In this instance, it is not that the victim is the romantic object of the sexually provocative stalk, but rather the reinforcement of the ego of the person with the Histrionic Personality Disorder. Unwilling to place second in the romance "contest," the person will engage in continuous stalking until the victim succumbs to her seductive behaviors. Commonly, upon winning the contest, the individual no longer wants the romantic relationship and seeks a new encounter.

THE NARCISSISTIC PERSONALITY

Persons afflicted with Narcissistic Personality Disorder believe that they are special and should be admired and sought out by others. "Individuals with this disorder generally require excessive admiration. Their self-esteem is invariably very fragile. They may be preoccupied with how well they are doing and how favorably others regard them. This often takes the form of a need for constant attention and admiration. They may expect their arrival to be greeted with great fanfare" (DSM-IV-TR, 2000, pp. 714–715).

The DSM-IV-TR continues in its description of the disorder. "Vulnerability in self-esteem makes individuals with Narcissistic Personality Disorder very sensitive to 'injury' from criticism or defeat. Although they may not show it outwardly, criticism may haunt these individuals and may leave them feeling humiliated, degraded, hollow and empty. They may react with disdain, rage or defiant counterattack" (p. 715).

Persons with this disorder are incapable of believing that someone can reject them. The act of rejection is incongruent with their Narcissistic Personality Disorder; therefore, it cannot and does not exist. The individual may engage in many behaviors to disprove this rejection. Expectations of sexual activity that are rejected are unacceptable. The person may force nonconsensual sexual activity upon the rejecting victim. Stalking behavior and subsequent assault are common. Rejected lovers and estranged and divorced spouses will follow the victim and confront her and any new suitors. Rejection is impossible to the person with Narcissistic Personality Disorder, who may resort to stalking conduct and assault to reverse the situation.

When threats of intimidation are not successful, the person afflicted with Narcissistic Personality Disorder will reverse the situation in order to maintain ego congruence, indicating that he was tired of this relationship and broke it off. The person may publicly degrade the other person and attempt to destroy her reputation.

THE ANTISOCIAL PERSONALITY DISORDER

The stalking conduct of the Antisocial Personality Disorder has serious implications. The DSM-IV-TR identifies many of the following characteristics that are common to the disorder and provide evidence of the potential for stalking conduct and violent behavior.

- Individuals with Antisocial Personality Disorder frequently lack empathy and tend to be callous, cynical, and contemptuous of the feelings, rights, and sufferings of others.
- They may repeatedly perform acts that are grounds for arrest such as . . . harassing others.
- Individuals with Antisocial Personality Disorder tend to be irritable and aggressive and may repeatedly get into physical fights or commit acts of physical assault (including spouse beating or child beating).
- They may be indifferent to, or provide a superficial rationalization for, having hurt, mistreated, or stolen from someone. These individuals may blame the victims for being foolish, helpless, or deserving their fate; they may minimize the harmful consequences of their actions or simply indicate complete indifference.
- These individuals may also be irresponsible and exploitative in their sexual relationships. They may have a history of many sexual partners and may never have sustained a monogamous relationship.
- Reckless disregard for the safety of self or others. (pp. 701–703)

The psychopathic nature of this disorder precipitates danger in the stalking pattern. The conduct of stalking by a person with Antisocial Personality Disorder is purposeful. It is willful and malicious in intent. These individuals stalk in order to precipitate fear and intimidation in their victim. They intend to make the victim fearful for safety and life. They are stalking particular individuals for whom they have specific intent. They may be stalking to produce fear as a mechanism of retaliation and control, or to dissuade a person from performing an activity. They may be specifically stalking for purposes of assault and willful murder.

The seriousness of the stalking conduct of a person with this disorder is severely exacerbated when it exists in a comorbid or dual diagnosis with a sexual paraphilia.

SEXUAL PARAPHILIAS AND STALKING

There is only one motivating factor that drives the stalking behavior of persons afflicted with sexual paraphilias—the generalized diagnostic criterion of recurrent, intense sexual arousal. The conduct of stalking for these people diverges in intent from the motivations discussed above. The stalking conduct of persons with sexual paraphilias may be directed at a specific individual or at a larger population. The population will represent the characteristics of the specific paraphilia.

Each of the sexual paraphilias will be examined for its probable patterns of stalking behavior, and each will be examined in the event that the paraphilia is found to be comorbid with another paraphilia and a personality disorder.

EXHIBITIONISM

Exhibitionism is when an individual has recurrent sexual arousal from the behavior associated with the exposing of his genitals to unsuspecting persons. If this behavior is not directed at a particular victim group, then the Exhibitionism is probably not comorbid with another paraphilia. The person is not intentionally stalking anyone, but rather is indiscriminately exposing himself to passersby. This individual derives pleasure from exposing himself to the victim and from the victim's subsequent shocked response. However, if the exhibiting of the genitals is only sexually arousing when targeting a specific group, then the stalking is purposeful, with a different intent.

The person who is sexually aroused when displaying his genitals to a prepubescent boy or girl may also be afflicted with Pedophilia. The recurrent, intense sexual arousal does not stem from his exposing himself, but rather from the fact that the victim is a child. The characteristics of the victim define the motivation for the exhibitionist behavior, and in this example, it would not be coincidental that the individual has chosen to locate himself near the commonly traveled paths of elementary school children. The pedophile chooses this location to expose himself because he expects his specific love interest or preferred age and gender group to travel here.

This exhibitionist behavior is not the paraphilia; it is a stalking pattern of a pedophile. When the pornography and masturbation no longer satisfy his intense sexual fantasies and urges, he ventures out of the privacy of his home to locate a child that fulfills his vision of his perfect lover. To find that perfect lover, he frequents locations where children fitting his age and gender preference are commonly found.

Recognizing this activity requires a new definition of the concept of stalking. The state statutes are explicit that the conduct must be directed at a particular individual and the victim must feel threatened, but the children of this victim group have no idea that they are being viewed and sorted out in the mind of the pedophile. It is analogous to the wild, hungry predator, such as a lion or tiger, that scouts the locations where its prey of choice is common. The predatory animal lies in wait to identify the perfect victim and then begins a premeditated stalk of its unknowing quarry.

Likewise, the pedophile visits locations where his preferred victim is commonly found, observes without being detected, and then identifies his perfect victim/fantasy lover. The observation alone is sexually arousing and may suffice, but only temporarily. The pedophile will return to his same hunting ground until he identifies his specific victim, and then he will begin a premeditated stalk.

The pedophile's exposure of his genitals may be directed at the general age/gender preference group or at his specific victim. The act of exposing himself to the target population may help him to identify his specific prey. Sitting in a car or in a park where children walk by, he may expose himself to age- and gender-relevant children. The pedophile may select his specific victim based on the child's reaction to his exposing himself. If the child screams and runs away, the pedophile will move on to a new location and a different group of children who possess similar characteristics.

However, if the child reacts with curiosity, the pedophile may feel he has identified his specific love interest. It is not necessary for the initial contact to continue; the pedophile will return to the same location to observe, follow, and perhaps even photograph his chosen victim. It is highly probable that the child has no idea that he is being observed, followed, or photographed. Thus, the behavior does not necessarily meet the statutory definition of stalking, even though the conduct of stalking is taking place.

It is critical that all episodes of Exhibitionism be reported to law enforcement officials, and more importantly, it is critical that officials carefully examine each episode to determine if the behavior is in fact part of a stalking pattern. It is also very significant to note that the fantasy love interests of stalkers are not just prepubescent children. The characteristics of the victim of the exhibitionist define the love interest of the exhibitionist. The victim's age and gender are primary indicators of the paraphiliac's love interests and fantasies.

Serial killer John Wayne Gacy murdered boys in their early teens. He was a hebephiliac whose love interests were teenage boys who had just recently arrived at sexual maturity. Gacy's pattern of stalking demonstrated his love interest. He would slowly drive the streets of downtown Chicago, where young gay boys could be found. He also frequented the Greyhound Bus station, watching for young males who had run away from their homes.

Jeffrey Dahmer readily admitted that he was looking for the most beautiful young men he could find. Dahmer stalked locations where beautiful, young gay men within a certain age group regularly congregated. He openly admitted to wanting to find a beautiful, young man who would be his lifelong lover.

With the exception of his final murders in Florida, Ted Bundy's victims looked remarkably similar. In order to locate his specific victim, he had to conduct a stalk of locations where young women would normally congregate.

Unless the exhibitionist behavior is an indiscriminate "flashing" of unsuspecting passersby, it is critical to examine the victim characteristics, as they will reflect the preferred love interest of the stalker. Individuals who expose themselves to particular victim groups generally do not switch to groups with different characteristics. That is, a person who exposes himself to elementary school-age boys will not subsequently be found exposing himself to a group of female college students. Similarly, the man who sits in the bleachers watching a college women's basketball team practice will not be found observing a group of elderly women doing aqua aerobics at the community pool. The victimology assists in determining the age, gender, and gender preference of the individual afflicted with one or more sexual paraphilias.

FETISHISM

Persons afflicted with Fetishism have intense, recurring, sexual arousal involving nonliving objects. The nonliving object, known as the fetish, that produces the sexual arousal is unique to the person afflicted with the Fetishism. Women's undergarments are commonly the fetish, but the DSM-IV-TR indicates that "this Paraphilia is not diagnosed when the fetishes are limited to articles of female clothing used in cross-dressing, as in Transvestic Fetishism, or when the object is genitally stimulating because it has been designed for that purpose (e.g., a vibrator)" (p. 570).

This DSM disqualifier implies that the fetish may be an object that is also associated with another paraphilia or directly associated with another individual. This differentiation is critical for considering whether the nonliving object is part of a pattern of behavior associated with another paraphilia.

The specific characteristics of the nonliving object provide clues to the potential for a comorbid paraphilia or that the act of possessing the nonliving object is a symptom of a different paraphilia. Searches conducted in the residences of arrested pedophiles and hebephiles commonly produce articles of clothing that are age- and gender-specific to the victim group. The garment is not the stimulus for the intense sexual arousal, but rather a prop used to enhance the fantasy.

It is also common to find articles of clothing that are possessions of the victim. The successful stalk of a group of age- and gender-preferred victims results in the identification of a chosen victim as the fantasy lover. The fantasy is significantly enhanced if the disordered person can obtain an article of clothing, preferably an intimate article of clothing, belonging to his fantasy lover. The stalking conduct has significantly increased in seriousness. He has gone from identifying a group, to the identification of an individual, to obtaining a piece of clothing belonging to that individual.

Obtaining the personal item of clothing is always an illicit activity. The stalker must follow the victim to his or her home, school, gym, or place of work. The possession of this garment is the last precursor behavior before contact. This nonliving object has the scent of his fantasy lover and it is as close to the victim's skin as he can get without actually touching it. Obtaining the garment is also a clandestine activity that is sexually arousing. The knowledge that he is close to the living space of his fantasy lover is overwhelmingly sexually arousing. The mere activity may produce heightened levels of anxiety that are distressing, but the reward overshadows the potential for being caught.

Rather than attempting an illegal entry into the victim's residence, the individual will look for other opportunities to obtain the desired object. This activity advances the stalking. A convenient opportunity to take an article of clothing is at the laundry facilities of a person who lives in an apartment or dormitory. The victim is not conscious that someone is watching her, waiting to take an item of her clothing, preferably an item that has not been washed and still holds her scent. Possessing an unwashed piece of the victim's undergarment is the ultimate treasure. The scent lingers and is utilized in the self-erotic behavior. Other items of clothing that are commonly taken include athletic warm-up suits that are put aside when athletes disrobe to practice and compete. They are commonly tossed on the sidelines or on the bleachers where they can easily be stolen while everyone else focuses on the activity.

Fitness clubs are an unending source of victims. People who join fitness clubs do so for more reasons than fitness. It is an opportunity to make social acquaintances, and for many it is the opportunity to view partially naked torsos of hundreds of men and women. It is a candy store for the sexual predator, an opportunity for the predator to find a group of age- and gender-preference victims and to view them discreetly, selecting his fantasy lover. In this environment, the stalking pattern moves along very quickly—it can move from group identification to individual identification and object retrieval in a single venture.

Many fitness clubs require that, following the use of a piece of exercise equipment, the exerciser wipes his or her sweat from the equipment as a courtesy for the next user. Fitness clubs provide towels for that purpose. Following the workout, the towels, drenched with sweat from the exercise, are thrown into a bag or bin for laundering. The unsuspecting victim discards a sweat-drenched towel, only to have it retrieved by the casually observing stalker. The stalker has his prize: a towel soaked in the sweat of his fantasy lover, sweat removed from the most intimate of locations.

Thus, the nonliving object is not merely a fetish that produces intense sexual arousal, but also a very intimate possession of the fantasy lover/victim. The intense sexual arousal is not based on the object but rather the victim who possessed it.

FROTTEURISM

People engaged in physically intimate relationships are commonly at different levels of receptivity to sexual activity, particularly at early stages in a relationship. The activity of kissing may produce sexual arousal for one or both of the persons, but advancing the physical intimacy to touching or petting may exceed the wishes of one of the parties. Forced petting is common. Touching and fondling may be pleasurable to both parties, but perceived social conventions may make one party reluctant to proceed at this time in the relationship. The reluctance may be temporary; continuation of the intimacy may increase the sexual arousal sufficiently for both parties to advance their intimacy. This advancement to fondling must be consensual. Otherwise it is considered nonconsensual, criminal sexual misconduct. Further, the determination of consensual is the perception of the person being fondled.

Frotteurism may exist as a singular diagnosis or may be comorbid with other paraphilias and personality disorders. Further, the behavior is not considered a paraphilia unless the behavior precipitates intense sexual arousal and social impairment. Teenage and young adult males may engage in grabbing the breasts or the buttocks of girls and women as a crude, sophomoric demonstration of their daring. While the behavior is offensive and illegal, it is probably not a manifestation of Frotteurism.

Conversely, the act of an elderly man who touches the breasts, thighs, or buttocks of a nonconsenting girl or woman should not be excused as the eccentricity of a "dirty old man." Whether the behavior constitutes a diagnosis of Frotteurism is insignificant; it is an act of criminal sexual misconduct, and the criminal justice system must intervene to dissuade recidivist behavior. If the conduct is excused or ignored, the behavior is reinforced and the individual will engage in it repeatedly until a consequence is applied.

The behavior must also not be diminished. The high school star athlete who fondles the female high school student must face the same consequences as the elderly man in the previous paragraph. Suggestions that the girl dressed seductively should not enter into the discussion. The seductive dress or mannerisms of the girl do not excuse the nonconsensual touching by the male student. Failing to present a consequence for the behavior has the dual effect of condoning the behavior and suggesting that girls who dress seductively are promiscuous and really want to be fondled.

Frotteurism is a valid diagnosis for those individuals who wait to ride the most crowded buses and subways and who are intensely sexually aroused by grinding their genitals into the unsuspecting stranger standing next to them. What appears as an innocent grabbing of a breast as one reaches for the upright support pole is often a commonly practiced behavior of the person afflicted with Frotteurism. Following the episode, the person takes the memory of the touch back to his home and relives it while masturbating. If the behavior is not rebuked, he may think the victim finds his touch pleasurable and will return the next day to locate the same victim.

Frotteurism may also be part of the stalking pattern of a specific victim. After the fantasy lover/victim has been located and observed from a distance, the paraphiliac's obsession to advance the relationship requires contact. Some predators will elaborately prepare what appears to be a chance encounter as a means to introduce themselves to their fantasy lover/victim. Bumping into the fantasy lover, knocking the packages or books from their arms, and then apologetically assisting them to pick them up may be a premeditated approach rather than a casual accident and opportunity to meet. Others find this direct method too anxiety producing and may attempt to advance their delusional romance by a nonconsensual touch.

People who frequent a fitness center will find themselves often touched by strangers—touches that appear quite innocent. Intense sexual arousal can be achieved for some afflicted people merely by touching the arm, shoulder, or hair of their fantasy lover. In contrast, a dark and very crowded dance floor is an ideal opportunity to rub one's genitals against an unsuspecting stranger. The victim dismisses the behavior as an inadvertent act caused by the crowded conditions, and the predator leaves with a fresh memory to add to his collection.

VOYEURISM

Voyeuristic behaviors differ in their degree and in their relationship to stalking. Voyeurism is in itself a definition of stalking; all voyeuristic behavior is a form of stalking. However, some forms of voyeuristic behavior are considerably more serious, are probably paraphiliac in nature, and may be part of a dangerous stalking pattern. If an individual is afflicted with the paraphilia of Voyeurism only, he still must seek out people to observe naked, in stages of undress, bathing, or engaging in sexual activity. This process of locating victims is stalking.

Persons engaging in voyeuristic behavior may also be found lurking in neighborhoods, drive-in movies, and abandoned areas locally known as "lovers lane." Locations such as these require courage to visit as the potential for detection and encounter is high. These individuals are aroused by the knowledge that the victim(s) is not aware of being observed. The clandestine activity may be as equally sexually arousing as the sight of flesh and sexual activity. This form of Voyeurism requires a premeditated stalk.

Evaluating neighborhoods for the prospect of Voyeurism requires a form of reconnaissance. Neighborhoods are selected not randomly but after careful examination. If the Voyeurism is comorbid with another paraphilia that is associated with a particular age and gender of preference, the neighborhoods will be examined for this population. If the voyeur has recurrent intense sexual arousal pertaining to college-age women, his voyeuristic activity will be conducted near women's college dormitories, sorority houses, and college apartment complexes. In contrast, if the individual is a pedophile, he'll seek out neighborhoods that offer availability of that age and gender group. If the individual is sexually aroused by fantasies of elderly women, his search will be limited to senior citizen communities. He may also secure employment at a nursing home, providing him extensive exposure to his victim population.

The reconnaissance will include a daylight visit to the neighborhood to ascertain the presence of the desired victim group. The presence of age- and size-relevant toys, bikes, and athletic equipment provides a clue to the age range of the inhabitants of the neighborhood.

Daylight reconnaissance also provides an evaluation of households that have dogs. The voyeur does not want his night excursion to be interrupted by a barking dog, or worse, to be attacked by the homeowner's dog. Houses are also examined for the presence of air-conditioning units. The windows of an air-conditioned house will be closed and the drapes drawn at night. The absence of air-conditioning units is a good sign that windows and curtains will be open, Daylight reconnaissance also provides the voyeur with information pertaining to window height, presence of fences and shrubs, and a place to park his vehicle where it will not be noticed. Close proximity of an all-night grocery store is an added advantage to the voyeur, because it's a convenient location to park his vehicle. A final nighttime reconnaissance mission, testing predetermined routes of entry and exit, prioritizes the neighborhoods and individual houses.

The undetected voyeur is as skilled at his conduct as is the successful burglar. His reinforcement for Voyeurism is the successful selection, stalk, and vision of persons in various stages of undress, bathing, or engagement in sexual activity. The memory is his prized possession. He will continue to visit the same neighborhood and houses as long as he feels his presence is undetected.

Considering that Voyeurism is, in effect, nonconsensual observing, other similar activities should be examined and considered as part of stalking conduct. Persons who have recurrent, intense sexual arousal pertaining to sexual activity with persons of a specific age and gender will locate groups of this desired population. Should this conduct not be considered stalking as well? The pedophile who watches young boys or girls play soccer, or the hebephile who watches cheerleaders practice is conducting voyeuristic stalking. The pedophile and hebephile are selecting fantasy lovers. While there is no guarantee that this activity will result in criminal sexual misconduct, it is appropriate to watch such people in return and question the appropriateness of their observation. They may simply enjoy watching children of a certain age playing, or their intent may be much more serious.

TELEPHONE SCATOLOGIA

In Chapter 4, the sexual paraphilia of Scatologia was discussed in depth. The behaviors of this paraphilia may also be part of the pattern of the stalking of an exclusive victim. Hearing the voice of a fantasy lover may be an intense sexually arousing experience for the stalker and he or she may call repeatedly just to hear the voice message of the fantasy lover. The predator may pretend to be a telemarketing agent with an unusual and outstanding offer that will engage the fantasy lover in a continued conversation. In contrast, if the intent of the stalk is to intimidate or threaten, he will either disguise his voice or say nothing. The stalker may use multiple locations and public phones in case the phone line is being tracked by the phone company or law enforcement. Further, it is common for stalkers who are unwilling to accept the loss of their relationship to wiretap the phone line of the victim to overhear conversations. The Indiana stalking statute acknowledges phone harassment in the definition of "impermissible contact." Specifically, the statute indicates "harassment means conduct directed toward a victim that includes, but is not limited to, repeated or impermissible contact that would cause a reasonable person to suffer emotional distress" (IC 35-45-2, Acts 1976, P.L.148 Sec 5). This definition acknowledges that phone harassment can cause a reasonable person to suffer emotional distress.

SADISM, MASOCHISM

Persons afflicted with Sexual Sadism or Sexual Masochism are generally involved in consensual relationships. These persons do not have to stalk their partners. There are bars, clubs, and organizations that cater to people interested in sadomasochism, and so these people can likely find a willing partner. Persons afflicted with one of these paraphilias and not interested in presenting themselves publicly will solicit prostitutes willing to participate in sadomasochistic activity. Married men and women who have an interest in sadomasochistic activity beyond the willingness of their spouse may turn to a prostitute in order to preserve their marriage and reputation while also meeting their sexual desires. The relationships are generally short lived, as the recurrent, intense sexual arousal is associated with either giving or receiving pain and humiliation.

PEDOPHILIA, HEBEPHILIA

The relationship of stalking patterns to Pedophilia and Hebephilia has been discussed at length in different contexts throughout this chapter and in previous sections of this book. The stalking pattern and mannerisms are directly related to the age and gender preference of the disordered person. As trite and obvious as this statement may appear, it is accurate. These leopards will not change their spots. Incarcerated pedophiles and hebephiles confess that their daily consciousness is overwhelmed with their fantasy of a love/sexual relationship with a child or youth of a particular age and gender. Detection will not change their fantasy victim population, just the location where they will stalk them.

Chapter 11

Sexual Assault, Rape, and Lust Homicide

This chapter is dedicated to the study of sexual assault, rape, and lust homicide. The subject matter of this chapter is explicit. Recognizing that the audience for this book is extremely varied, from grandparents to law enforcement officers and all parties in between, this author will describe the illicit actions of sexual predators in terms that are found in common use, while at the same time defining clinical and legal terms for the edification of the reader.

It is significant to reiterate that there is no empirically established direct correlation of a diagnosis of a sexual paraphilia to rape and/or lust homicide. Individuals who experience recurrent, intense sexual arousal as defined by one of the sexual paraphilias may seek professional assistance to deal with the paraphilia and yet *never* engage in nonconsensual activity. However, the correlation is relatively absolute in reverse. Specifically, although there is no guarantee that indicates a person afflicted with certain sexual paraphilias will commit nonconsensual sexual assault, persons who do commit nonconsensual sexual assault commonly are afflicted with a sexual paraphilia.

On the opposite side of the coin, some sexual assault, even to the extent of rape, may be committed by persons who are not afflicted by a sexual paraphilia, or, in other words, who are not experiencing recurrent, intense sexual arousal as defined by any of the paraphilias. This chapter will attempt to delineate sexual assault, rape, and lust homicide originating in sexual paraphilias and identify those assaults that may take place *without* a clinical disorder.

SEXUAL ASSAULT

The term "assault" has varied definitions, which appear in law and common usage. Statutes defining assault differ from state to state with disparate degrees of severity. Some states consider the usage of vulgar language as verbal accosting and assault, categorizing it in their criminal code as a misdemeanor. Other states consider the threat of harm as an assault and register it as a criminal violation. Therefore, the reality of sexual assault is contextual. While most states may statutorily acknowledge that nonconsensual intercourse forced by a husband upon his wife is legally considered rape, the processing and prosecution of the offender may be arbitrary and contingent upon the personal opinion of the responding law enforcement officer and/or prosecuting attorney.

Regardless, the victim was sexually assaulted. Complaints of domestic violence are commonly sexual assaults. Jurisdictions that fail to remove the burden of formal complaint from the victim also fail to acknowledge the victim's fear of retaliation for filing the complaint. When domestic partners are forced into sexual activity without consent, they become victims of sexual assault, and the state should assume the responsibility as the complainant. Domestic partners who are dependent upon the assaulting party for their welfare and the welfare of their children are fearful of filing complaints and the subsequent loss of economic security.

Sexual assault must be carefully examined pursuant to motivation. As with stalking taxonomies, sexual assault and rape cannot be clearly delineated and categorized. The motivation for sexual assault is unique to the perpetrator. Failure to recognize the individuality of motivation reduces the significance of the assault. This is particularly significant in relation to stranger sexual assault. The motivation for acquaintance assault is more clearly recognized. Prior intimacy, marriage role expectations, and control are common motivations for acquaintance sexual assaults. The greatest majority of sexual assaults are acquaintance assaults; consequently, the perpetrator is readily identified. The acquaintance assault is no less significant, particularly to the victim for whom recidivism is an expectation; however, stranger assault adds "a stranger" to the equation.

Stranger assault takes on a different perspective from acquaintance assault. Again, this is not to reduce the significance of acquaintance sexual assault, but to stick to the objective of this book, which is to reduce the incidence of stranger sexual assault—both the initial episode and, particularly, repeated offenses. There are different motivations that precipitate stranger sexual assault. The motivation is important to understand and for deterring sexual assault.

Numerous authors have established taxonomies of sexual assault and rape pursuant to motivation. However, categorization implies a finite number of motivations that precipitate sexual assault. In reality, the motivation for sexual assault is as unique and authentic as the person who commits the assault. It is critical, therefore, to examine a variety of assaults that may or may not have their etiology in sexual paraphilias.

Persons who commit sexual assaults and who do not experience recurrent, intense sexual arousal pertaining to a particular victim or aspect of sexual activity are probably not afflicted with a sexual paraphilia. In such a case, the sexual assault is not precipitated by a clinical disorder. Numerous motivations for sexual assault, rape, and homicide are not precipitated by paraphilias. The motivation—such as that found in domestic violence—is commonly identifiable in the activity of the crime scene.

Some sexual assault is motivated by peer pressure and a desire to be acknowledged and accepted. This is particularly true in the multiple or "gang" rape of a victim. Men participating in group activity demonstrate a pack behavior that is similar to that found in the animal kingdom. Acceptance into a group of male peers is overwhelmingly important to adolescent and post-adolescent males. These males have no interest in personal authenticity; they want to appear in all aspects just like the rest of their companions. Men dress alike for acceptance from their peers and do not desire to stand out in a crowd.

Males conform to the behavior expectations of their peer groups, and particularly the dominant individual in the group. Similar to the alpha male of a wolf pack, the dominant male directs the activity of the male peer group. It is common for this alpha male to be an Antisocial Personality Disordered or Narcissistic Personality Disordered individual. Their egocentricity requires that they be the center of attention and the leading force in the peer group. This characteristic is readily observed in small groups of males. Two dominant males cannot occupy the same social space, as it is incongruent to their egos. The dominant one will prevail by requiring the members of his intimate group to perform behaviors that they would not normally perform as individuals. One demonstration of supremacy by the alpha male and compliance by the other members may be a gang rape of a stranger. Other demonstrations of loyalty and willingness to belong, such as auto theft, shoplifting, consuming quantities of alcohol or drugs, and physical fights do not demonstrate the level of loyalty as much as rape and murder do.

Other sexual assaults without a clinical etiology include raping a person who happens to be inside an auto that is being carjacked, or raping the clerk of a store that is being robbed. The rape is a subsequent thought, secondary to the primary objective of the car theft, armed robbery, home invasion, and so on.

In further discussion of the motivation for sexual assault, the conduct may be consensual, but the victim is *legally* incapable of consenting to the activity, which makes it statutory rape. Every state has established an age of consent, and disparity in this age exists from state to state. Young men and women below a state statutorily-prescribed chronological age cannot consent to sexual activity. Regardless of the precocious, sexually mature appearance and the willingness of the youth to participate in sexual activity, if his or her chronological age falls below the age of consent, it is considered criminal sexual conduct and rape if intercourse has taken place.

Many college-age males have been charged with statutory rape because sexually precocious high school females have attended fraternity parties pretending to be college students, and therefore old enough to consent to sexual relations. The precocious appearance and nature of the victim and her willingness to participate does not reduce the culpability of the perpetrator, but these may be considered mitigating factors during sentencing.

As noted earlier in the book, unattended young women fall prey to men, individually and in small groups, who utilize "rape drugs" to engage in sexual activity with the anesthetized victim. Rape drugs can be easily slipped into young woman's drinks and the subsequent drug reaction renders her susceptible to nonconsensual sexual activity. The drug not only reduces the victim's ability to ward off sexual activity, it also has an amnesiac affect, so when the victim awakens the next morning and experiences the pain associated with forced intercourse, she is completely incapable of remembering the previous night's events. Finally, the perpetrator's use of a condom reduces the possibility of a DNA analysis.

STRANGER ANGER RAPE

Another nonparaphiliac-associated stranger sexual assault is related to anger and aggression. In contrast to the sexual assault directed at a particular acquaintance for purposes of control, intimidation, or retaliation, anger-related stranger sexual assault is linked to the displacement of the anger from another person or situation. A man who is angry with his supervisor may not vent his anger directly at the supervisor, fearing job loss. Instead, he may choose to vent his anger in the form of road rage, bar fights, spouse and child abuse, and, occasionally, stranger rape.

The stranger anger rape can be displaced anger from an acquaintance woman to a stranger victim. Angry with his wife, girlfriend, mother, or female supervisor, the rapist may choose a stranger woman on whom to vent his anger and aggression. It is also a strong possibility that victims are chosen because they are weaker and less capable of inflicting retaliatory injury during the assault. This type of rape is characterized by very violent behavior in which it is obvious that the primary intent is to inflict injury, not to achieve sexual intimacy.

Because the intent is to inflict injury, the perpetrator may use a weapon or an implement in the process of committing the rape. He will batter the victim with force that is beyond what is necessary to control the victim. If the victim resists or attempts to fight back, the attacker will increase the violence and death may result. Unless there is a striking resemblance between the victim and the source of the rapist's anger, the victims are generally randomly chosen. The infamous serial killer Ted Bundy chose victims that closely resembled a young woman from his past who had romantically rejected him. In Bundy's case, he was premeditatedly stalking women who met this criterion.

Most cases of stranger anger rape are not premeditated. Rather, the victim is chosen by availability and opportunity. Angry and drunk, the stranger rapist finds a young, unattended, and inebriated woman a likely victim. If she leaves the bar unescorted, the angry male may follow her to the parking lot, force her into the vehicle, pummel her into submission or unconsciousness, and rape her.

Stranger anger rape is not limited to heterosexual activity. Young gay men are also the victims of anger-displaced sodomy. However, episodes of this nature may be related to hate crimes. Homophobic males may violently assault gay men as a mechanism to vent their anger.

SEXUAL PARAPHILIAC ASSAULT AND RAPE

The premise that a sexual assault or rape may be precipitated by a sexual paraphilia assumes that the assault is sexually motivated. The previous discussions described sexual assaults, rape, and murder that are motivated by anger and not sexual arousal.

To reiterate the criteria for a sexual paraphilia, "the essential features of a Paraphilia are recurrent, intense sexually arousing fantasies, sexual urges, or behaviors generally involving 1) nonhuman objects, 2) the suffering or humiliation of oneself or one's partner, or 3) children or other nonconsenting persons. . . . For some individuals, paraphiliac fantasies or stimuli are obligatory for erotic arousal and always included in sexual activity" (DSM-IV-TR, 2000, p. 566).

The sexual assault of a stranger also creates a second premise: The person committing the assault does not have the availability of a consensual partner, or the sexual activity with the consenting partner is not meeting the recurrent sexual urges, fantasies, or behavioral desires of the person committing the assault. If this and the criteria described above are present, we can then be certain that the motivation for the assault is the intense paraphilia.

The previous chapters thoroughly delineate the criteria and the behavioral manifestations of the various paraphilias. If the driving force behind a sexual assault is a paraphilia, the relevant behavioral manifestations will be observable in the assault.

Sexual Sadism

The sexual sadist cannot achieve sexual arousal unless he is inflicting psychological or physical pain and suffering on a victim. As a consequence, the victim will experience differing levels of humiliation and torture contingent upon the severity of the sadism paraphilia of the person committing the assault. The rapist may use derogatory terms, slap, bite, and perhaps even mutilate the victim. However, it is significant to note that the emotion of anger is absent. Unlike the anger rapist discussed above, this rapist is desirous of achieving sexual arousal, which is dependent on the delivery of pain and suffering. The attacker is also sexually aggressive in the delusional belief that the victim likes his or her sexual activity rough. It is not the intent to kill the victim, but sometimes the victim's vigorous resistance to the rape will elicit increased aggressive behavior that may result in death. In essence, it is a catch-22 for the victim—if the victim is compliant, the attacker will increase his aggressiveness in order to achieve his sexual arousal; if the victim vigorously resists, it communicates to the attacker that she does indeed like her sex rough and he will increase the intensity of the attack.

Victims of these attacks are less random because the attacker premeditatedly stalks a particular type of victim to meet his fantasy image. Jeffrey Dahmer looked only for the most beautiful young, gay men within a certain age range. He did not have any racial or ethnic preferences. He stalked beauty.

Attackers, intent upon aggressive sex, are commonly sexual sadists who have been rejected from the mainstream sadomasochistic community because of their penchant for extreme violent sex. They stalk particular areas where sexual masochists congregate and solicit prostitutes for "kinky," aggressive sexual activity. The sexual sadist who must resort to stranger sexual assault will carry a "kit" with him as he stalks his victim. Handcuffs, duct tape, silk scarves, and rope may be found in the kit. The kit may also contain sexual paraphernalia commonly associated with sadomasochist consensual activity and other sources of pornographic material readily available at adult bookstores. The specific behavior demonstrated in the course of the rape reflects the characteristic criteria of the sexual sadist.

Pedophiliac and Hebephiliac Assault and Rape

Pedophilia and Hebephilia are demonstrated in the age of the victim. Other characteristics of the assault are more common with prepubescent and pubescent victims than with older victims. Characteristic of pedophiles and hebephiles is the delusion that the child loves them as much as they love the child. The disordered person believes that once the child meets and gets to know him, the child will love him equally in return. This paraphilia, in contrast to the other paraphilia, is based on a love fantasy.

Pedophiles and hebephiles do not define their conduct as a sexual assault or attack. In their minds, they are attempting to develop a loving, intimate sexual relationship with the child. Further, they do not find the conduct morally repugnant. They have no interest in hurting the child, only in loving the child. When the child resists the advance, the disordered person, who is now clutching his love fantasy, is intensely sexually aroused and begins to force the child into sexual activity. Pedophiles, in particular, may never achieve intercourse with the child. Restraining the child and muffling his or her screams while attempting to fondle the child may result in premature ejaculation. It is common to find the semen of the attacker on the clothing of the child. The attacker is so intensely aroused that he ejaculates before there is any opportunity for intercourse.

It is the screams of the child or the child's threats of telling his or her parents that results in the death of the child. It is never the intent of the pedophile. His motivation is to secure the lifelong love of the child, not to injure or kill. Children who have been killed in sexual assaults are found to have significant bruising around the mouth. The child has died from asphyxiation; in an attempt to quiet the victim, the attacker smothered the child. In addition, if a child threatens to disclose the identity and action of the attacker, he or she may be killed and the body disposed of in hopes of hiding the crime and the attacker's identity.

Children at puberty and adolescence are the prey of the hebephile. Their larger size requires higher degrees of control. Adolescents are more capable of fighting back and when it becomes obvious to the hebephiliac that his sexual advances are not welcome, the child may be struck, or otherwise restrained. Recognizing that he is unable to intimidate the child into subsequent silence, he murders the child. Again, the interest lies not in injuring or killing the adolescent. Like the pedophile, the hebephile is attempting to form a lifelong loving relationship with the victim. Unlike the pedophile, the hebephile is more apt to accomplish intercourse with the victim. The subsequent death of the adolescent is to preserve the attacker's identity.

The etiology of both Pedophilia and Hebephilia is attributed to the fact that such people themselves were victimized children. If a child grows up in an environment where he receives nurturing, love, and affection in the form of sexual contact with a significant other, he will consider such inappropriate sexual activity an expression of love. If the molestation continues and is not corrected, the child may adopt this behavior pattern for his own expression of love and affection. Rather than kiss his younger brother or sister on the top of the head, he will fondle the child's genitalia.

Obviously, not all molested children grow up to be pedophiles or hebephiles. Most child victims of sexual abuse mature into adults who are capable of a healthy, age-appropriate sexual relationship. However, a small percentage does not and remains fixated on sexual fantasies about children or adolescents. These disordered persons' sexual interests arrested at the stage in their development when the sexual activity was associated with love and affection. Frequently incapable of attaining and maintaining age-appropriate sexual relationships, they revert to a time in their lives when they felt safe, secure, and loved. This phenomenon is exemplified in their response to anxiety in their lives.

Feelings and expressions of human sexuality in non–sexually disordered persons are indirectly related to stress levels. As levels of stress increase, non–sexually disordered persons are less apt to feel and express their sexuality. As stress reduces and comfort returns, their feelings and expressions of sexuality increase.

In contrast, pedophiles and hebephiles experience a direct correlation between levels of stress and expressions of sexuality. "The behaviors may increase in response to psychosocial stressors" (DSM-IV-TR, 2000, p. 568). Pedophiles and hebephiles, unable to achieve age-appropriate sexual relationships, experience psychosocial stressors that cause them to revert to the activities in their lives that they remember as anxiety free. They recall the warmth and love of their sexual activity as a child, and thus develop the delusion that somewhere a child exists who will love them unconditionally in return. Rather than face their inadequacies in age-appropriate intimate relationships, they look to find a child or adolescent to love them equally.

COMORBIDITY

More than one paraphilia may be diagnosed in the same person, or the behavioral manifestations of other paraphilias may be part of a progressive pattern of behavior. A person diagnosed as a pedophile may manifest symptomatic behaviors of Exhibitionism, Fetishism, Frotteurism, and Voyeurism. The specific paraphilia is not intensely sexually arousing to the pedophile, only the fantasy lover is. The pedophile may demonstrate characteristic criteria of other paraphilias, but they are a part of the progressive pattern of behavior, beginning in the privacy of the pedophile's home and ending with the selection of a "live" fantasy lover.

Paraphilias may also be comorbid with personality disorders and the manifested behavior will indicate both the personality disorder and the paraphilia. The serial murderer John Wayne Gacy demonstrated the behavioral criteria of Antisocial Personality Disorder, Hebephilia, and Sexual Sadism. Gacy stalked adolescent males, engaged in sexually sadistic behavior with them, and murdered and buried them in the crawl space under his house in suburban Chicago. His serial murders demonstrated the same patterns, as well as his lack of remorse and conscience deficiency characteristic of the Antisocial Personality Disorder.

It is important to emphasize that the motivation for sexual assault, rape, and lust homicide is unique to the attacker. Any attempt to bundle them up in a tidy taxonomy is neither successful nor useful. The motivations are as unique as the persons who commit the assaults. Therefore, each episode of assault requires a careful examination to identify the precipitating motivation.

Chapter 12

Prevention, Prediction, and Apprehension of Predators

Logic dictates that the most successful way to reduce sexual assaults is to prevent them in the first place. Sexual assaults, rape, and lust homicides can be prevented based on understanding the relationship between the sexual paraphilias and assault patterns. It is not necessary to wait for the child to be abducted or the young woman to be raped for society to legally and legitimately intervene.

There is no concrete evidence that all persons afflicted with a sexual paraphilia will assault another person. However, under the premise that sexual assaults are motivated by recurrent, intense sexual arousal pertaining to a sexual paraphilia, sexual assaults can be examined for behavioral manifestations that are unique to specific sexual paraphilias. If a child is sexually assaulted, the motivation precipitating the assault is most likely the age and gender of the victim. If a person is apprehended masturbating while peeking into a stranger's home, one may conclude that the behavior was precipitated by the intense sexual arousal associated with watching a person disrobe, bathe, or engage in sexual activity.

The conduct would not take place if there were no sexual motivation to precipitate it. The characteristics of the conduct exemplify the motivation. The nonconsensual act of grabbing a woman's breast demonstrates that the behavior was conducted because it was intensely sexually arousing to the person committing the attack. However, it is significant to recognize that the specific pattern may also be part of a pattern of conduct associated with a different and more serious paraphilia. The grabbing of a woman's breast may be indicative of Frotteurism. If the victim is a 13-year-old girl and the attacker is a grown man, it is likely that the act of grabbing the prematurely developed breast was associated with Hebephilia rather than Frotteurism. The attacker was probably intensely sexually aroused by the age of the victim rather than the act of nonconsensual touching. Intentionally observing pubescent-age girls play in a playground rather than watching scantily dressed mature women work out at the fitness center indicates the observer's preference.

The behavior would not be performed unless there was a reason for it. The man watches the age and gender group of preference and is satisfied. If it were not satisfying, he would not do it. It is possible that he is a grandfather who is geographically removed from watching his grandchildren participate in athletic events. If the observing is repeated and repeated, then one must question the motivation. It is simple: The act of observing is pleasurable, and it fulfills the disordered person's needs.

Finally, it must also be recognized that the apparent paraphiliac behavior may actually be part of a progressive stalking pattern. The alleged paraphilia does not precipitate the intense sexual arousal; the victim fantasy group does. The behavior of observing pubescent girls may be symptomatic of Hebephilia. The victim's age and gender group is the stimuli. In the future the mere act of watching and remembering his visions may not suffice. It may be necessary for him to take an item of clothing, follow her home, exhibit his genitals to her, attempt a nonconsensual touch, or draw up a plan to introduce himself. In a premeditated plan to find his fantasy lover, the pedophile may carry a puppy in his arms. He then can deceive the child, requesting her help in finding the owner of the little dog.

If the behavior is symptomatic of a more serious paraphilia and part of a progressive pattern of stalking, one can expect the behavior to intensify and become more individualized.

PREVENTION

Recognition of sexual paraphilias as precursor behaviors on the continuum leading to direct contact with the fantasy love object is the first step in preventing sexual assault. The second step is determination of the victim group. Children and adolescents are not the only victim groups of sexual predators. Women of all ages, gay men, and minorities are victim groups of sexual predators. With the exception of prison populations, heterosexual males are not commonly considered targets of sexual predators.

Because of her naiveté, a woman may fail to recognize the precursor behaviors of a sexual predator. A woman frequenting a coed fitness club considers men's glances and stares as complimentary, without any consideration of her potential to be a victim of a sexual predator. The chance meeting of a fellow classmate or work associate miles from her common ground is considered coincidental. Finding her car parked next to a fellow classmate or worker at a shopping mall is laughed off as coincidental. At some point, the irrational thoughts of coincidence vanish, and the dark reality of being stalked is recognized.

Unsolicited phone calls or e-mail cards and driving by the residence constitute stalking. The sexual predator finds pleasure in his behavior and will continue it. Adults must be observant of coincidence in their daily lives. It is understandable that children and adolescents are not particularly aware of their surroundings, but adults do possess the cognitive ability to be observant.

Adults have the responsibility of watching out for children and adolescents. Every child or adolescent that has been abducted, sexually assaulted, and murdered was given instructions to avoid strangers. Because children and adolescents cannot be instructed in all of the possible scenarios that a sexual predator may utilize to achieve his goals, it is the responsibility of adults to watch out for the children. Children who are carefully watched are less apt to be abducted.

Adults watch the children, but they fail to remain alert for the persons who are also observing the children. Visit any elementary playground at recess and you will find teachers, principals, and aides on duty. They stand with their backs to the fence while the children play inside the secure area. They should be positioned so that they can observe outside the secure area to see who is watching the children play. Bus drivers should be aware not only of the children getting on the bus, but also any unfamiliar vehicles parked nearby. Crossing guards and bus drivers should be instructed to write down the license plate numbers of any unfamiliar vehicles positioned near the school, and principals should report this information to local law enforcement officers.

Parents attending age-group athletic events watch their children compete, but they never scan the crowd of spectators for an unfamiliar face.

The little league soccer field or swim team is fertile ground for the pedophile and hebephile. Parent organizations need to find a volunteer parent to video the sidelines at every practice, match, or meet. Comparing the faces on the video with known parents excludes nearly everyone from suspicion. The unknown parties are then compared to the photos of registered sex offenders in the community and the video is made available to local law enforcement.

Parents, coaches, and teachers should also scrutinize the staff. Finding a male college student to volunteer as an assistant soccer coach is met with unbridled enthusiasm rather than measured skepticism. Why does a college student in his mid 20s want to volunteer his free time to coach soccer to elementary girls and boys? His motivation may be perfectly innocent, but the hard, embarrassing questions need to be asked. Are all volunteer Big Brothers asking for an assignment out of the goodness in their hearts? Is the college student who volunteers to assist with the Boy Scout troop just interested in scouting, or is he stalking? Adults need to question the motivation of persons working with children and adolescents.

PREDICTION

Two significant issues pertain to the prediction of the behavior of sexual predators. True sexual predators do not change their age and gender preferences. As a leopard does not change its spots, neither does the sexual predator change his fantasy lover preference. Like the leopard, he may, however, change his stalking territory.

When a sexual predator has found a viable target group, he will continue to stalk that group until the potential for his detection increases. The pedophile will work the same elementary school playground until the principal, teachers, aides, and bus drivers start to observe the persons who are watching the children. This novel thought will drive him away as quickly as the unexpected arrival of a police car. He will move to a new school, one that does not implement the program of watching the watchers. He will not change the age and gender preference, just the territory.

On a rainy day or a day when school is not in session, the sexual predator moves to the indoor shopping mall or the theater that is showing the current animated movie. He will lodge himself down unobtrusively across from the children's play area and pretend to be reading a newspaper. He will fill his eyes with the potential of fantasy lovers and will continue to return on rainy days until the mall security officer questions him regarding his activity. The reinforcement for the behavior is high, but the consequence for being detected override his desire to stay and he will move to new territory.

Therefore, if an incident of Exhibitionism takes place, you can predict it will happen again, perhaps not in the same location, but definitely to a similar age and gender victim population. If a man exposes his genitalia to a young boy in a bathroom at a mall, fearing detection, he probably will not return to the same location. However, he will offend again. He will locate another bathroom in a mall, city park, beach bathhouse, or other public venue to expose himself to a similarly aged boy.

The second significant issue pertaining to prediction is the escalation of behavior. If the misconduct is symptomatic of a more serious paraphilia, one can predict that the behavior will increase in severity, frequency, or both. Just as a drug addict requires more and more of his chosen drug to get high, the initial stimulus for the sexual predator will begin to lose its potency and he will have to increase the frequency of the behavior or escalate it along his disordered continuum. What may start as mere observation of the chosen victim group may turn to following, touching, or stealing personal items.

The sexual assault, rape, or lust homicide is the final assault. Precursor behaviors indicated the individual's paraphilia and preferences. It is critical to recognize the behavior as a precursor to a more serious behavior and, when legitimately possible, to intervene.

APPREHENSION

Responding after the abduction, attack, rape, or lust homicide is too late. The act has taken place and we have a victim of a rape or lust homicide. The criminal codes of every state describe criminal sexual misconduct at all levels of severity, from Voyeurism to lust homicide. Assault, rape, and lust homicide can be prevented by the apprehension, prosecution, and sentencing of sexual predators at the less serious levels of criminal sexual misconduct.

Voyeurism and Frotteurism are violations of the criminal code and prosecutorial action must be taken. The behaviors cannot be excused as the prank of some high school kids or the action of a "dirty old man." Each incident of sexual misconduct must be examined as a potential precursor behavior of a serious paraphilia that may result in a more serious sexual assault. This is not to say that incarceration is the requisite consequence; mental health treatment may be the sentence of choice. However, it is significant that the behavior is acknowledged as a violation of law and the sexual predator, upon a finding of guilty, be subjected to psychological evaluation for the existence of a sexual paraphilia.

Society's failure to demand complete enforcement of the criminal code and the prosecution of offenders condones criminal sexual misconduct and sentences its victim populations to more incidences of sexual assault, rape, and lust homicide.

Bibliography

American Psychiatric Association (2000). *Diagnostic and statistical manual of mental disorders* (4th ed., Text Rev.). Washington, DC: Author.

Ansbacher, H. L., & Ansbacher, R. R. (Eds.). (1956). *The individual psychology of Alfred Adler.* New York: Basic Books.

Atkins, M. C., McKernan, M., & Talbot, E. (1996). DSM-4 Diagnosis of conduct disorder and opposition defiant disorder: Implications and guidelines for school mental health teams. *The School Psychology Review, 25*(3), 274–283.

August, G. J., Realmuto, G. M., Crosby, R. D., & MacDonald, A. W. (1995). Community-based multiple-gate screening of children at risk for conduct disorder. *Journal of Abnormal Child Psychology, 23*(4), 521–524.

Bandura, A. (1977). *Social learning theory.* Englewood Cliffs, NJ: Prentice Hall.

Bartol, C. R. (2002). *Criminal behavior: A psychosocial approach* (6th ed.). Upper Saddle River, NJ: Prentice Hall.

Belknap, J. (1996). *The invisible woman.* Belmont, CA: Wadsworth.

Binder, A., Geis, G., & Dickson, B. (2001). *Juvenile delinquency* (3rd ed.). Cincinnati, OH: Anderson.

Blinder, M. (1985). *Lovers, killers, husbands and wives.* New York: St. Martin's Press.

Burack, J. A., Hodapp, R. M., & Zigler, E. (1998). *Handbook of mental retardation and development.* Cambridge, UK: Cambridge University Press.

Burgess, A. W. (Ed.). (1985). *Rape and sexual assault.* New York: Garland.

Buzawa, E. S., & Buzawa, C. G. (2003). *Domestic violence* (3rd ed.). Thousand Oaks, CA: Sage.

California Penal Code. Statute Title 15. Chapter 2. Section 646.9. Retrieved March 29, 2004, from http://www.law.cornell.edu.

Chandler, J. (1999). In *Oppositional defiant disorder and conduct disorder in children and adolescents: Diagnosis and treatment.* Retrieved March 29, 2004, from http://www.klis.com/chandler.

Cohen, A. (1955). *Delinquent boys.* New York: Free Press.

Colt, G. H. (1998). Were you born that way? *Life, 21*(4), 38–42.

Crespi, T. D., & Rigazio-DiGilio, S. A. (1996). Adolescent homicide and family pathology: Implications for research and treatment with adolescents. *Adolescences, 31,* 353–367.

Crowell, N. A., & Burgess, A. W. (Eds.). (1996). *Understanding violence against women.* Washington, DC: National Academy Press.

Day, H. D., Franklin, J. M., & Marshall, D. D. (1998). Predictors of aggression in hospitalized adolescents. *Journal of Psychology, 132*(4), 427–434.

Deary, I. A., Peter, A., & Austin, E. (1998). Personality traits and personality disorders. *The British Journal of Psychology, 89*(4), 647–661.

Dobbert, D. L. (1981, January). *Profiling and predicting the violent offender.* Paper presented at the meeting of the National Conference on Serious and Violent Offenders. Detroit, MI.

Douglas, J., & Olshaker, M. (1997). *Journey into darkness.* New York: Simon and Schuster.

Douglas, J. E., Burgess, A. W., Burgess, A. G., & Ressler, R. K. (1992). *Crime classification manual.* San Francisco: Jossey-Bass.

English, K., Pullen, S., & Jones, L. (1996). Managing adult sex offenders: A containment approach. *American Probation and Parole, 13*(1).

Eysenck, H. J. (1977). *Crime and personality.* London, UK: Routledge.

Eysenck, M. W., & Keane, M. T. (1995). *Cognitive psychology* (3rd ed.). East Sussex, UK: Psychology Press.

Flora, R. (2001). *How to work with sex offenders: A handbook for criminal justice, human service, and mental health professions.* Binghamton, NY: Hayworth.

Florida Penal Code. (2003). Statute Title XLVI. Chapter 784.048. Retrieved March 29, 2004, from http://www.law.cornell.edu.

French, M. (1992). *The war against women.* New York: Simon and Schuster.

Glasser, A. J., & Zimmerman, I. L. (1967). *Clinical intepretation of the Wechsler Intelligence Scale for Children.* New York: Grune and Stratton.

Glueck, S., & Glueck, E. (1950). *Unraveling juvenile delinquency.* Cambridge, MA: Harvard University Press.

Goody, E. (1977). *Deviant behavior* (5th ed.). Upper Saddle River, NJ: Prentice Hall.

Gosselin, D. K. (2003). *Heavy hands* (2nd ed.). Upper Saddle River, NJ: Prentice Hall.

Groth, N., Burgess, A., & Holmstead, L. (1977). Rape, power, anger and sexuality. *American Journal of Psychiatry, 134,* 1239–1243.

Hare, R. D. (1970). *Psychopathy: Theory and research.* New York: Wiley.

Hare, R. D. (1980). A research scale for the assessment of psychopathy in criminal populations. *Personality and Individual Differences, 1,* 111–119.

Hasslet, V. B., & Hersen, M. (1999). *Handbook of psychological approaches with violent offenders: Contemporary strategies and issues.* New York: Kluwer.

Hazelwood, R. R., & Warren, J. (1989). The serial rapist. *FBI Law Enforcement Bulletin,* 49–63.

Hinman, L. M. (Ed.). (1996). *Contemporary moral issues.* Upper Saddle River, NJ: Prentice Hall.

Hodgson, J. F., & Kelley, D. S. (2001). *Sexual violence: Policies, practices, and challenges in the United States and Canada.* Westport, CT: Praeger.

Holmes, R. M., & Holmes, S. T. (2002). *Profiling violent crimes* (3rd ed.). Thousand Oaks, CA: Sage.

Horney, K. (1950). *Neurosis and human growth.* New York: Norton.

Indiana Penal Code. (2002). IC 35-45-2, Acts 1976, P.L. 148 Sec 5. Retrieved March 29, 2004, from http://www.law.cornell.edu.

James, S. H., & Nordby, J. J. (Eds.). (2003). *Forensic science.* Boca Raton, FL: CRC Press.

Kaye, D. H. (1997). *Science in evidence.* Cincinnati, OH: Anderson.

Keeney, B. T., & Heide, K. M. (1994). Gender differences in serial murderers. *Journal of Interpersonal Violence, 9*(3), 383–398.

Klein, E., Campbell, J., Soler, E., & Ghez, M. (1997). *Ending domestic violence.* Thousand Oaks, CA: Sage.

Klotter, J. C., & Edwards, T. D. (1998). *Criminal law* (5th ed.). Cincinnati, OH: Anderson.

Knight, R. A., & Prentky, R. A. (1987). The developmental antecedents and adult adaptations of rapist subtypes. *Criminal Justice and Behavior, 14,* 403–426.

Lane, B., & Gregg, W. (1992). *The encyclopedia of serial killers* (Rev. ed.). New York: Berkeley.

Magid, K., & McKelvey, C. A. (1987). *High risk.* Toronto, Canada: Bantam.

Masters, W. H., & Johnson, V. E. (1966). *Human sexual response.* Boston: Little and Brown.

Medows, R. J. (2001). *Understanding violence and victimization* (2nd ed.). Upper Saddle River, NJ: Prentice Hall.

Memon, A., Vrij, A., & Bull, R. (1998). *Psychology and law.* Berkshire, UK: McGraw Hill.

Nathanson, D. L. (1992). *Shame and pride.* New York: W. W. Norton.

National Center for the Analysis of Violent Crime. (1992). *Investigator's guide to allegations of "ritual" child abuse* [Brochure]. Quantico, VA: Author.

National Center for the Victims of Crime. (2001). *The national women's study.* Retrieved July 5, 2002, from http://www.ncvc.org.

New Jersey Penal Code. (1994). Megan's Law-NJSA.2C:7-1 through 7-11, L.1994, c.128. Retrieved March 29, 2004, from www.law.cornell.edu/topics/state_ statutes.html.

Nordby, V. J., & Hall, C. S. (Eds.). (1974). *Practice and theory of individual psychology.* San Francisco: Freeman.

Olsen, J. (1974). *The man with the candy.* New York: Simon and Schuster.

Peled, E., Jaffe, P. G., & Edleson, J. L. (Eds.). (1995). *Ending the cycle of violence.* Thousand Oaks, CA: Sage.

Piaget, J. (1967). *Six psychological studies.* New York: Random House.

Rolling, D., & London, S. (1996). *The making of a serial killer.* Portland, OR: Feral House.

Rowe, D. C. (2002). *Biology and crime.* Los Angeles: Roxbury.

Sadler, A. E. (1996). *Family violence.* San Diego: Greenhaven Press.

Schwartz, M. D. (Ed.). (1997). *Researching sexual violence against women.* Thousand Oaks, CA: Sage.

Sgarzi, J. M., & McDevitt, J. (2003). *Victimology.* Upper Saddle River, NJ: Prentice Hall.

Shaw, C. R., & McKay, H. D. (1972). *Juvenile delinquency and urban areas.* Chicago: University of Chicago Press.

Sheldon, W. (1949). *Varieties of delinquent youth.* New York: Harper Brothers.

Stark, A., & Flitcraft, A. (1996). *Women at risk.* Thousand Oaks, CA: Sage.

Steinberg, L. (1999). *Adolescence* (5th ed.). Boston: McGraw Hill.

Stolzenberg, L., & D'Alessio, S. J. (Eds.). (2002). *Criminal courts for the 21st century* (2nd ed.). Upper Saddle River, NJ: Prentice Hall.

Sutherland, E. (1947). *Principles of criminology* (4th ed.). Philadelphia: Lippincott.

Van Wormer, K. S., & Bartollas, C. (2000). *Women and the criminal justice system.* Needham Heights, MA: Allyn and Bacon.

VanderZanden, J. W. (1997). *Human development* (6th ed.). New York: McGraw Hill.

Warren, J., Reboussin, R., Hazelwood, R. R., & Wright, J. A. (1991). Prediction of rapist type and violence from verbal, physical, and sexual scales. *Journal of Interpersonal Violence, 6*(1), 55–67.

Websdale, N. (1998). *Rural woman battering and the justice system.* Thousand Oaks, CA: Sage.

Webster's unabridged dictionary (2nd ed.). (2001). New York: Random House.

Wedding, D., & Boyd, M. A. (1999). *Movies and mental illness.* Boston: McGraw Hill.

Weisheit, R. A., & Culbertson, R. G. (2000). *Juvenile delinquency* (4th ed., Rev.). Prospect Heights, IL: Waveland Press.

Weston, P. B., & Wells, K. M. (1997). *Criminal investigation* (7th ed.). Upper Saddle River, NJ: Prentice Hall.

Wrightsman, L. S. (2001). *Forensic psychology.* Belmont, CA: Wadsworth.

Index

About the Author

DUANE L. DOBBERT has more than thirty years' experience working in the field of Criminal Justice. He is a diplomate of the American Board of Forensic Examiners and a diplomate of the American Board of Psychological Specialties. He has been a consultant for hundreds of law enforcement, judicial, and corrections agencies in the United States. He is also a professor at Florida Gulf Coast University and Capella University.